The Morgan Affair And Anti-Masonry

John C. Palmer

PREFACE

ACKNOWLEDGMENT is freely made of the writer's indebtedness for the material gathered into this booklet, to many instructive and exhaustive studies by other Masons into this same subject. Notable among these works, all to be found in the Library of the Scottish Rite in the House of the Temple in Washington, are—Robert Morris's "William Morgan"; Charles McCarty's "The Anti-Masonic Political Party" (very full and satisfactory); Peter Ross's "The Morgan Craze" (which gives a very useful bibliography of the subject) and many others. For the strongest presentation of the Anti-Masonic side of the question, the letters of John Quincy Adams and William L. Stone, with the Autobiography of Thurlow Weed, may be consulted.

JOHN C. PALMER.

INTRODUCTION

IT would be pleasant if the roadway could lead always along the sunlit heights of unbroken favor and good fortune. But experience teaches that frail mortals always sooner or later find the path dipping down into the valley; with its winding curves, its alternating ascents and descents, its darkening shadows.

Rarely does a river find its way to the sea in even, steady, unbroken flow. There is first a downward rushing torrent; then a backward sweeping eddy; then a series of rapids; the waters hurtling themselves against hidden rocks, dashing on with furious sound and foam, until at last, the deep full-channelled stream is reached that sings its quiet way to the sea.

History is a record of alternating successes and failures, advances and retreats of men and nations and institutions. True, through the ages one increasing purpose runs and the law of progress is the law of life. But that purpose usually attains its fulfillment along a tortuous way; progress is achieved only after many a strenuous conflict.

We are to study together one of the backward eddies in the Masonic stream; one of the hidden rocks against which our craft was dashed, imperiling its very life; one of the shadows of the valley, dark, threatening, full of foreboding.

Innumerable pamphlets and books have been published relating to the Morgan incident and describing the activities of the Anti-Masonic Party which grew out of the subsequent furore. Almost without exception, they are violently partisan. To the most casual reader they betray their bias. It will be difficult, but it ought to be possible at this date so far removed from the controversy, to discover the facts, to sift out the truth from this mass of contradiction, to put the whole movement in its proper setting; and so to gain some profit, if such there be, from this sombre incident of Masonic History. First of all, then, a brief review of the social, political and economic events of that first half century of the American Republic.

CONTENTS

		PAGE
I	Fifty Years of Progress in the American Republic	1
II	Story of William Morgan	13
III	The Abduction	20
IV	The Aftermath	29
V	The Anti-Masonic Party	38
VI	Conditions in New York State	49
VII	Anti-Masonry in Pennsylvania	65
VIII	Anti-Masonry in New England	78
IX	The Secrecy of Masonry	89
X	Masonry Survives the Storms	96
XI	Some Reflections	114

THE MORGAN AFFAIR AND ANTI-MASONRY

CHAPTER I

1776—1826

FIFTY YEARS OF PROGRESS IN THE AMERICAN REPUBLIC. MASONRY KEEPING STEP IN GROWTH AND SERVICE

THE Colonies with unmatched heroism had made their Declaration of Independence. The Constitutional Convention under the leadership of Washington, Hamilton and Madison had wrought out the Constitution of the United States and it had been adopted and put into execution (1789). A peaceful republican government had been established. The staunch, incorruptible Washington had stood firm and unmoved amid all the tempests of opinion during that period of organization. The brilliant Hamilton, genius of governmental finance, had been spared to establish the government on a sound financial basis, ere he had been cut down by the bullet of Aaron Burr. From the day when John Marshall (Jan. 31, 1801) was commissioned Chief Justice of the Supreme Court, the people were assured of interpretation of law and constitution, clear, authoritative, and unquestioned. To the wise diplomacy of Franklin and Jefferson was added that brilliant stroke of Livingston who secured from Napoleon the vast empire west of the Mississippi known as the Louisiana Purchase.

The importance of this acquisition was scarce realized at the time. Nor had any public man, so far as it appears, any prescience of the far-reaching advantage which this country had gained, when by this single stroke of diplomacy, she secured for every child, an inheritance which in other lands would be possible to the first-born only; virtually offering to every man who would accept it, a share in the public domain. The most important feature in the life of the Republic of that first decade of the century, was the rapid development of this western empire.

Jefferson commissioned two officers of the army, Meriwether Lewis and William Clarke, to explore the great North-West. They traced the course of the Missouri River for 2,600 miles; they crossed the Continental Divide and discovered the two streams which bear their names; followed them until their junction in the Columbia which they traced on to the sea. Evidence of the steady, consistent growth of the nation is found in the carving, out of the older territory, of eleven new states to be added to the original thirteen. These new states were, Vermont, 1791; Kentucky, 1792; Tennessee, 1796; Ohio, 1802; Louisiana, 1812; Indiana, 1816; Mississippi, 1817; Illinois, 1818; Alabama, 1819; Maine, 1820; and Missouri, 1821.

Meanwhile the population increased from three and

one-half million to thirteen million. In his flattering prophecy of the greatness of the new nation, much quoted at the beginning of the century, the Abbe Raynal had fixed ten million as the maximum population that might be hoped for. Wealth was increasing in even greater proportion. Following Whitney's invention of the cotton gin in 1793, the exports of cotton rose from 189,000 pounds to 83,000,000 in 1820. Sugar was brought from the West Indies to American ports and reshipped to the countries of Europe, in single years the exports reaching 400,000,000 pounds. The Napoleonic wars kept Europe constantly dependent on American importations and literally forced trade on fortunate American merchants.

This greatly increased commerce stimulated the building of American ships. The earliest statistics available are of the year when the Constitution went into effect (1789). In twenty years this tonnage had multiplied three-fold. It was inevitable that so lucrative a trade should excite the jealousy of other nations. International Law was not any too well defined. Irritating incidents at sea were frequent and hot-tempered commanders were apt to interpret them as insults to the flag of the new nation. War with France was narrowly averted. Jefferson was accused of favoring that Government with whose revolutionary philosophy he was so sympathetic. Controversies with Great Britain were most frequent because her navy was largest, her trading vessels most numerous, and hers the commerce which we had supplanted.

John Jay, in 1794, negotiated a Treaty with England covering the right of search, the impressment of seamen, and other questions that caused frequent conflict between commanders of British and American vessels. But, on his return with this treaty for submission to the President, so strong was the feeling, he was burned in effigy in the streets of New York. In 1806, Monroe and Pinckney negotiated still another treaty covering the same points; but Jefferson refused to submit it to the Senate. During Madison's first term, the sense of violated rights could no longer be restrained and Congress by a sharply divided vote declared war.

From 1812 to 1815 the war was waged on the ocean, along the Canadian border, on the Great Lakes and along the lower Mississippi. While results were indecisive, America drew great comfort from the showing of her infant navy in contest with the ships of the Mistress of the Seas; Commodore Perry won undying fame in the battle of Lake Erie; while the greatest honors on land went to Gen. Andrew Jackson for the Battle of New Orleans: won by his sturdy, keen-eyed militia, recruited from the farms and forests of the West, against the trained veterans of the best armies of Europe. Henry Clay, John Quincy Adams, James A. Bayard and Jonathan Russell were appointed commissioners to treat with commissioners from England. They met at Ghent and after five months of discussion arranged terms which were approved by the President. The joy of the people at news of peace was unbounded.

Matters of domestic concern soon pressed for attention of statesmen. The war had cost $100,000,000 in money; it had interfered with the shipment of cotton from the south, and with all the trade and commerce of the New England states. Banks, excepting those in Boston, suspended specie payments; paper currency was at a large discount and the business of the country consequently disarranged. A new national bank was chartered, with increased capital and enlarged powers. The tariff was readjusted to give protection to American manufactures and industry. These measures brought some relief though they could not prevent a critical period of depression which brought widespread loss.

All the while the question of slavery kept intruding itself. Should new states and territories be free or slave? The admission of every new state brought on a fresh conflict. Webster and Calhoun led the contending forces in the Senate; while Clay attempted the part of mediator. His Missouri Compromise bill (1821) seemed for a time to offer a peaceful solution. By its provisions, Missouri was admitted as a slave state, but all other territory west of the Mississippi and north of the southern boundary of Missouri was to be forever free.

Thus there were serious problems of foreign and domestic policy to divide the suffrages of the people and to arouse strong and even bitter antagonisms between differing sections of the Union. But on the whole after fifty years experience, a permanent government had been established. It had grown steadily in population, in added states, in wealth. It had shown itself able to contend successfully on land and sea with one of the great powers of the world; and to settle by majority vote of its citizenry, questions of vital import, concerning which differing opinions were strongly held. Thus Europe's sneering doubts that such a republic permanently could live and prosper seemed to be answered definitely in the affirmative.

Masonry Keeping Step with the Republic

Bro. Joseph E. Morcombe, Past Grand Historian of Iowa, has a striking sentence, "The sky line of history shows Masonry not as a central structure of its time, dwarfing all other structures; but it does show a notable edifice, strongly constructed and designed for very definite purpose." That fairly measures the institution of Freemasonry during the half century under consideration. No one can understand the force that sustained and maintained the Revolutionary cause in that long unequal struggle of the feeble colonies with the greatest power of Europe, who is ignorant of the far-reaching, tenacious fidelities of this fraternity that binds into a common brotherhood the commanding general of the army with the humblest private of the ranks.

Masonry had been transplanted from Europe in the early colonial period. Boston and Charleston were the first centers, though dispensations granted by the two Grand Lodges of England had provided charters for lodges in widely scattered localities. In 1734 Henry Price, a merchant of Boston, received appointment as Provincial Grand Master over all America under British rule. Within a year he had issued warrant for a lodge in Philadelphia appointing Benjamin Franklin its first Master. A year later a lodge was organized at Charleston, South Carolina. The Order grew constantly until it covered the whole country as is evidenced by the following list of Grand Lodges. Massachusetts: St. John's Lodge organized 1733; Ancient, 1769; The United Grand Lodge, 1772; Virginia, 1778; Maryland, 1783; Pennsylvania, Georgia, New Jersey, 1786; South Carolina, 1754, 1787; North Carolina, New York, 1787; Connecticut, New Hampshire, 1789; Rhode Island, 1791; Vermont, 1794; Kentucky, 1800; Delaware, 1806; Ohio, 1809; District of Columbia, 1811; Louisiana, 1812; Mississippi, 1818; Maine, 1820; Missouri, Alabama, 1821; Illinois, 1823; Michigan, 1826 (reorganized 1844).

Masonry's membership included many of the leaders of the Revolution. It is a matter of common fame that most of the signers of the Declaration of Independence, had knelt at Masonic altars. Gen. Joseph Warren, whose untimely death at the Battle of Bunker Hill was said by Gage (the British General) to be worth that of five hundred ordinary rebels, was Grand Master of Masons of the State of Massachusetts. Almost without exception, the officers entrusted by Gen. Washington with important posts were Master Masons. Washington, himself, was made a Mason in Fredericksburg, Va., on November 4, 1752. On February 3, 1783, the Grand Lodge of Pennsylvania chartered a lodge at Alexandria, Virginia (near his Mt. Vernon home), to be known as Alexandria No. 39. A few years later this lodge transferred its allegiance to the Grand Lodge of Virginia, to be known as Alexandria No. 22. Subsequently in 1805, it took the name of Washington Alexandria Lodge No. 22. Its time-stained charter still hangs on the wall of the lodge room in Alexandria bearing its mute, conclusive testimony that General Washington was a charter member and first Master of the Lodge.

During his entire life, The Father of his Country quietly, unostentatiously acknowledged his Masonic relationship. At his first inauguration, the oath of office was taken over a Bible from the Altar of St. John's Lodge of New York City. He laid the cornerstone of the Capitol with Masonic ceremonies. The gavel which he used is still preserved and treasured by Potomac Lodge No. 5 of Washington, D. C., which was the original Lodge of Georgetown and participated in the cornerstone ceremonies. As late as 1797 Washington addressed the Grand Lodge of Massachusetts in these words: "My attachment to the Society of which we are members will dispose me always to contribute my best endeavors to promote the honor and prosperity of the Craft."

Benjamin Franklin, whose wisdom and integrity enabled him to render service to his country in her darkest hour of need which secured to him the highest honors a grateful country could bestow, was an active Mason, Master of his Lodge and Provincial Grand Master. In France and in America he counseled freely with his brethren on the true principles of life and character. Considering his heavy official duties, his faithful attendance on Masonic engagements was extraordinary.

John Marshall became a Mason early after reaching his majority and continued his affectionate attachment to the fraternity until his death. The elevation of Marshall to the bench of the United States Supreme Court as Chief Justice marked an epoch in the legal and constitutional history of the United States. For thirty-four years he dominated the Court by his great learning and masterful power of analysis. His service on the bench was effective in securing for the Court profound respect; and also, in so expounding the Constitution as to make clear, for the first time, the relationship of the three Departments of the National Government and to forecast the lines of judicial interpretation along which the Nation was to proceed. At a notable gathering of Masons in Washington City, March 9, 1822, called to consider the propriety of establishing a General Grand Lodge of the United States, Justice Marshall was present and expressed his sentiments in behalf of Freemasonry in affecting terms.

Henry Clay was another of the leaders of his day, who was active in Masonry. He received the Masonic degrees in 1789 and served as Grand Master of Masons of Kentucky during 1820–21. Though he failed to reach the Presidency, Clay's attractive personality and brilliant eloquence drew to him a large personal following and made him a striking character of his generation. An address delivered by him at Lexington, Ky., December 27, 1802, fairly scintillates with gems of Masonic thought. Its peroration is: "Masonry through life is a never-failing source of happiness and consolation. Occupied in contemplating the beauties of the creation, in cherishing and cementing the great principles which bind us to our fellowmen, enraptured with the harmony and order to be seen in all the works of Nature, the soul of the Mason is elevated until he feels an irresistible disposition to gratitude and admiration of the Grand Master of the Universe. And when the awful hour of death itself arrives, it is disarmed of its terror by the reflection that the last sad office of mortality is performed by Brethren, whose slow and sober gait is traced by the tear of the most affectionate of ties."

Still another notable Mason of the period was De Witt Clinton, builder of the Erie Canal, Governor of New York, leader in establishing the free school system of New York City. Tom Corwin was another Grand Master of Masons who attained distinction in the state. As Governor of Ohio, as United States Senator, and as Secretary of the Treasury in President Fillmore's Cabinet, he rendered distinguished service.

Then there was Andrew Jackson, Grand Master of Masons of Tennessee, who maintained his devotion to the Order to the last. He won distinction by his victory over General Pakenham at New Orleans. Defeated in his first contest for the Presidency, in 1828 he was chosen seventh President of the United States. During the eight years of his administration he ruled with an autocratic independence that is still a tradition of his party. His Presidency covered the years of the violent Anti-Masonic agitation. Yet even in the midst of it, his devotion to the Order was expressed in his customary forcible terms. He assured the Grand Lodge of Massachusetts that he should ever feel a lively interest in the welfare of an institution with which he had been so long connected, and whose objects were purely philanthropic. During the very fury of the strife President Jackson wrote this open letter to the Grand Lodge of the District of Columbia, in reply to an invitation to be present at the laying of the cornerstone of a church in Alexandria, Va.:

Washington City, March 27, 1830.

Respected Sir:

I regret that the duties of my office will not allow me to avail myself of your polite invitation ***. It would afford me the highest pleasure to unite with my Masonic Brethren in laying the cornerstone of a religious edifice proposed to be built in Alexandria, and in marching afterward to the tomb of Washington. The memory of that illustrious Grand Master cannot receive a more appropriate honor than that which Religion and Masonry pay it, when they send their

votaries to his tomb fresh from the performance of acts which they consecrate. I am very respectfully,
ANDREW JACKSON.

Here then, at the end of the first half century of the Republic, Masonry had twenty-six Grand Lodges; governing an aggregate of three thousand constituent Lodges; whose membership may be reckoned at one hundred and fifty thousand men. When the Marquis de La Fayette made his historic visit to the United States in 1824, which developed into a triumphant tour of our cities, he found the most distinguished men of the day gathered in the Masonic Lodges. Again and again in response to their words of welcome, he addressed them in his characteristic fashion; short, terse, full of thought. This sentence is culled from one of these addresses: "Freemasonry is an order whose leading star is philanthropy, and whose principles inculcate an unceasing devotion to the cause of religion and morality."

Masonry had kept step with the growth of the Republic. Its members had rendered conspicuous service in the state. Its membership included ministers of religion, statesmen, officers and men of the Army and Navy, merchants, artizans, farmers, citizens of the highest and humblest ranks. They had given fullest proof of their patriotism and their devotion to the best interests and welfare of mankind.

Then came the Morgan incident.

CHAPTER II

STORY OF WILLIAM MORGAN

DURING the years 1824–1826, there lived in Batavia, New York, one William Morgan, who sometimes worked as a brick-mason. He had a wife and one child and in 1825 a second child was born. He was a man without property or means; never maintained a home for his family but boarded with one family or another convenient to his work. He had come to Batavia from Rochester in 1824; to Rochester from Canada in 1823; to Canada from Richmond, Virginia, in 1821. In his long and patient quest for information as to the life and character of Morgan, Robert Morris visited a man who was distantly related to Morgan, a Mr. E. S. Ferguson of Ulrichsville, Ohio, who gave him these facts. Morgan was born in Culpeper County, Virginia, August 7, 1774. He married Lucinda Pendleton in October, 1819, and two years later moved to York, Canada, and began business as a brewer. Another relative, John Day of Gordonsville, Kentucky, told Morris that Morgan served his apprenticeship as a brick-mason with Day's brother at Hap Hazard Mills, Madison County, Virginia. After reaching his majority, he emigrated to Kentucky, returning to Virginia four years later to work on the Orange County Court House. It was then that he married and moved on to Canada.

Samuel D. Greene who traversed New England during the later years of his life as an Anti-Masonic lecturer, is Morgan's most favorable biographer. In his "Broken Seal; or Personal Recollections of the Morgan Abduction and Murder," he gives a glowing picture of his hero. He says, "Captain Morgan was my friend and neighbor, and I was in free and daily intercourse with him. He was a man of fine personal appearance, about fifty years of age, of remarkable conversational powers, so that he was everywhere known as a good talker. He was a native of Virginia and was by trade a bricklayer, but for several years before coming to Batavia had been otherwise employed. He was a soldier in the War of 1812, and brought his title of Captain from the army during that war. He had served under General Jackson at New Orleans, and was a man of fine soldierly bearing. He was gentlemanly and agreeable in his manners. In later years the Masons charged him with being a drunkard, but in my judgment without reason. He was a convivial man, and at times would drink freely, according to the fashions of the day. I have myself seen him when he had been drinking more than was good for him; but he was not what, in the general acceptation of the word at that time, would be called a drunkard. It was the period of hard and general drinking, and certainly it ill becomes Freemasons to charge men on this score; for no body of men among us have done more, from generation to generation, to promote drinking habits than they."

Greene 'captained' Morgan and 'coloneled' Miller, his partner in the publishing of the exposé; but the evidence is clear that neither was entitled to any military title. Greene defended the correctness of the title, claiming that the Commission authorizing it was among the papers seized by the Masons at the time of Morgan's arrest. The War Department records, which should be final, fail to show any service by Morgan.

In contrast with Greene's glowing commendation, Morris quotes from his notebook (which contains his report of interviews with more than a hundred persons who knew Morgan personally), such comments as these: "a worthless fellow," "low down white trash," "bankrupt," "an habitual liar," "a hanger-on at grog shops," etc. All this testimony led Morris to classify him as a sot, a bummer, an ignoramus.

Somewhere between these extremes, the truth lies. Let us say that the evidence justifies the opinion that Morgan was a shiftless itinerant, a rolling stone that gathers no moss; more or less fond of his drink; without any considerable schooling, yet with some natural gifts; else he would not have been welcomed into so many lodges as visitor to assist in the conferring of degrees, nor as speaker and entertainer at special Masonic functions. He must have been a man of presentable appearance, of plausible manner and speech; else he could not so have imposed on staid, intelligent men of unblemished reputation. That he soon wore his welcome out, evidences his lack of substantial character. His carelessness in meeting his financial obligations would quickly undermine the confidence of new friends. His arrests for debt, aside from the charges used to get him into the hands of those who were determined to drive him from the country, were numerous and unquestioned. His idleness and improvident habits often left his family in sore straits which were relieved by grants from the Masonic charity funds.

His Masonic relations are strangely clouded. The record is clear that he was exalted to the Royal Arch degree. The original entries on the records of Western Star Chapter R. A. No. 33 of LeRoy, New York, are as follows:

February 15, 1825.—Voted that William Morgan's petition be entered on file.

April 12, 1825.—Voted that the ballot be passed for William Morgan. Past and clear.

May 31, 1825.—William Morgan, Israel Rathbone and Beach Defores were duly prepared and exalted to the degree of Royal Arch Masons.

The ledger of the Chapter of the same date has this entry:

William Morgan $12.
Israel Rathbone $12.
Beach Defores $12.

But no records have ever been found to indicate where he received the degrees required to make him eligible for the Royal Arch. Judge Ebenezer Mix, a veteran Mason of Batavia and a man of high repute, who followed the Morgan affair with critical eye from first to last, gave this explanation of the matter. In 1823 Morgan worked in Rochester as a brick-mason for a Mason named Warren. He so won the confidence of Warren as to persuade him that he (Morgan) was a Freemason; and accordingly was vouched for and enabled to visit a lodge in Rochester and afterward Wells Lodge No. 282 at Batavia. He claimed to have been made a Mason in Canada where the work is somewhat different from that in New York and so he diverted suspicion that might have been aroused by his stammering attempts to pass examination. Judge Mix continues: "Some yet living, explain how he got the Royal Arch degree. That he declared on oath that he had regularly received the other six degrees and thus satisfied the Chapter brethren at LeRoy." Judge Mix makes this comment, "There must have been a most reprehensible laxity among the Masons both of Rochester and of LeRoy; for there was no evidence educed, then or afterwards, that he had ever received any Masonic degree save the Royal Arch on May 31, 1825 at LeRoy."

After his removal to Batavia, it was said that Morgan became one of a class that met to receive instruction from the Grand Lecturer, Dr. Blanchard Powers. Dr. Powers always denied this; but in some way Morgan familiarized himself with parts of the ritual and came to have a certain reputation for the ease and impressiveness with which he rendered these parts. His dramatic style, his social disposition, his willingness to assist, caused him to be in some demand in lodges of neighboring towns. When in 1825, it was determined to apply for a charter for a Royal Arch Chapter at Batavia, he was one of those approached and gave his signature to the application.

There had been a growing suspicion in the minds of some as to his Masonic regularity; Blanchard, Powers and Abelard Reynolds are named among others who doubted: and his careless habits and financial looseness and neglect of his family, had determined some of the brethren to object to Morgan as a member of the new Chapter. His name was dropped from the application, and when the Charter was received and the Chapter instituted, much to his chagrin he found himself outside. This led to a quarrel with some of the brethren whom he held responsible for his omission. It began to be whispered about that Morgan was preparing a betrayal of the ritual and secrets of Freemasonry. In the Spring of 1826 he filed with the Clerk of the northern district of New York application for copyright for the book to be written. Its title was given: "Illustrations of Masonry by one of the Fraternity. *God said let there be Light and there was Light.*" News of this intended publication went from Lodge to Lodge all through Central New York, and aroused a deep feeling of resentment. Sober minds counselled absolute silence, advising against any action against Morgan. They predicted that if let severely alone, the book would fall stillborn. September 1, 1826, ten days before Morgan's disappearance, the Batavia *Spirit of the Times* published a letter from Henry Brown (a Mason) in which he strongly deprecated the indiscreet excitement of some Masons, as well as the violent asperity of the enemies of the Order. "No man in his sober senses," said he, "can credit the perjured wretch who commences his career by publishing his infamy. The attempt has often been made before and always has proven abortive, terminating in disgrace to those concerned."

On March 13, 1826, Morgan entered into a contract with David C. Miller, John Davids and Russell Dyer for the publication of his exposé. Miller had a printing office and since 1811 had published the Batavia *Republican Advocate*. Twenty years before, he had taken the Entered Apprentice Degree at Albany, N. Y.; but his lodge having refused to advance him further, he had cherished his grudge against the Institution and waited his opportunity to inflict injury upon it. It was at the home of John Davids that Morgan was boarding at the time. Russell Dyer lived in Rochester, N. Y., and no information is available concerning him. They were men of small means. On August 5 of that year these three partners executed a bond in the penal sum of $500,000, guaranteeing to pay to Morgan one fourth of the expected profits. Morgan was now industriously at work, preparing the manuscripts for his book. With cheerful defiance he would, from time to time, announce in the bar-room or on the street, the progress he was making. Feeling ran high and the determination rapidly formed that the publication must be prevented at whatever cost.

CHAPTER III

THE ABDUCTION

ON Monday, September 11, 1826, Holloway Hayward, a constable of Canandaigua, New York, arrested Morgan on a warrant sworn to by Ebenezer Kingsley, a tavern-keeper of Canandaigua. He charged Morgan with the theft of a shirt and cravat taken five months before. Hayward was accompanied by a posse of six men and the arrest caused some excitement. Miller, the publisher, loudly protested the removal of Morgan beyond the Genesee County limits. The constable insisted on taking his prisoner according to the warrant. He offered to return by way of LeRoy (within the county) to permit Morgan to plead before Squire Foster there, where bail could be given for his appearance at the next Court of General Sessions at Canandaigua. But Morgan preferred to go direct to Canandaigua, for he thought he could convince the tavern-keeper that he had not stolen the shirt but only borrowed it.

On his arraignment at Canandaigua, he was examined and at once acquitted of the charge of larceny; only to be immediately rearrested on an execution issued by the Coroner for a debt of $2.68, and jailed for inability to meet the debt. On the evening of Tuesday, September 12, he was released on payment of the debt by another party and at once departed in a coach with several other persons. There was some commotion as he entered the coach, his hat was lost and it is evident he did not go entirely of his own will. He was later traced to Ft. Niagara, where he was confined in an unused magazine. Here all definite trace of the man ends, though many varied conflicting and unconfirmed accounts have been published of his reappearance in Syria as a merchant, in Mexico as a derelict, in the West as an Indian Chief and in Australia as leading an industrious and exemplary life.

His disappearance caused instant and widespread indignation. Governor Clinton, himself a Past Grand Master of Masons, issued three successive proclamations dealing with the matter. In the first, dated October 4, 1826, he writes that sworn information has been presented to him by a committee of citizens, representing that divers outrages and oppressions have been committed on the persons or citizens of the village of Batavia. He urges all good citizens to cooperate with the authorities to maintain the ascendency of law and order.

On October 26, he issued a second proclamation stating that Morgan had still not been found and offering a reward for any information leading to his recovery or to the conviction of those who had spirited him away. A third proclamation appeared on March 19, 1827, offering a reward of two thousand dollars to the end "that if living, Morgan might be returned to his family; and if murdered, that the perpetrators might be brought to condign punishment." He also offered free pardon to any accomplice who should make full discovery of the offenders. He denounced it as "a crime abhorrent to humanity and derogatory to the ascendency of law and good order."

Rigorous investigation disclosed the fact that certain Masons had arranged for the changes of horses and drivers for the 125 mile journey from Canandaigua to Ft. Niagara. All who had any part in the arrest at Batavia, the release at Canandaigua, and the conveyance to Ft. Niagara were relentlessly prosecuted. Special Attorney-Generals were appointed by the Governor to conduct the prosecution and the aroused sentiment of the state should have made convictions easy. Chesebro, Lawson and Sawyer (all Masons), who were members of the posse accompanying the Constable who made the arrest, pleaded guilty to indictments charging them with conspiracy to seize and secrete Morgan and were sentenced to terms in prison. Eli Bruce, Sheriff of Niagara County, was removed by Governor Clinton, convicted of aiding in the conspiracy, and served two years in prison. He had arranged for one stage of the journey and had ridden in the coach with Morgan. John Whitney was convicted of conspiracy and served eighteen months in the county jail.

Desperate efforts were made to prove the murder and to convict Masons as the murderers; but the inability to locate the body made it impossible. A year later, that is on October 7, 1827, a man's body was washed ashore at the beach of Oak Orchard Harbor,

New York, about forty miles below Ft. Niagara. The published notice of the Coroner's inquest, giving "death by drowning" as the verdict, brought a party of Batavians to the scene. The corpse was disinterred October 13 and a second inquest held on Monday, October 15, 1827. The widow, though she admitted the clothes were not the same her husband had worn when he left home, expressed her belief that the body was that of Morgan. Miller, Russell Dyer and others testified to the same effect. Thurlow Weed, Editor of a Rochester paper, who was to take such a prominent part in fostering the Anti-Masonic Party, was present and his course of action was the basis of long and bitter controversy. Morgan had a bald head and smooth face with peculiar long white hairs in his ears and nostrils. The corpse had a heavy beard and full head of hair. Before the inquest began, so the accusation went, Weed had the bearded corpse shaved, and hairs plucked from the forehead and thrust into the ears and nostrils. The verdict was rendered that the corpse was that of Morgan.

But the publicity incident to this inquest, brought to the scene the friends of one Timothy Munroe, of the township of Clark, District of Newcastle, Upper Canada. It seems that on September 24, 1827, while returning in a row boat from the American side, the boat upset, he was thrown into the water and drowned. His widow, Mrs. Sara Munroe, came to Oak Harbor, the seat of the original inquest and her minute description of the clothing worn by her husband and the marks by which he might be identified, tallied so accurately with the description of the body that a third inquest was made decidedly advisable. A Coroner's jury, impanelled at Batavia, heard her story; reversed the former verdict and decided that the corpse was that of Munroe.

But as months passed without Morgan's return, the charge of murder was more insistent. Many stories were circulated giving in detail how certain Masons were chosen by lot and met at the Ft. Niagara Magazine and took Morgan in a boat to the center of the river and pushed him overboard to his watery grave. Thurlow Weed from his death bed in New York in 1882 addressed a sworn statement to the N. Y. *Sun*, declaring that in 1860 in Chicago, John Whitney (one of those convicted of conspiracy to seize and secrete Morgan) had confessed to him that he with four other Masons, after the plan to have Morgan confined by Canadian Masons had failed, took him in a boat at midnight, bound him hand and foot, fastened a weight about his body, rowed to the middle of the Niagara River, forced him overboard, then silently rowed to the shore and without a word separated and went to their respective homes. Weed said that it was agreed that he was to reduce the confession to writing and to take it to Whitney for his signature; but that Whitney died before he had opportunity to attend to it.

As a matter of fact, Whitney lived until 1869 and was buried by Masons in Graceland Cemetery in Chicago. His son-in-law, who was present at the interview with

Weed, strenuously denied that any confession was made; that instead, Whitney was so enraged at seeing his longtime and bitter accuser, that he could scarce be restrained from a personal attack on Weed.

Whitney's story to Robert Morris was that he and Chesebro, alone, were responsible for the plan of removing Morgan: though a number of others were asked to assist in the undertaking. Incensed at Morgan's treachery, he had gone to consult with Governor Clinton at Albany. The Governor sternly charged him that there must be no steps taken that would conflict with a citizen's duty to the law. He counselled the purchase of the Morgan manuscripts; and, if his consent could be secured, his removal to some locality beyond the knowledge and influence of Miller and his other associates in the enterprise. Whitney was assured of a supply of money up to a thousand dollars if needed. He then visited Batavia, stopping at the Danold Tavern. Morgan was sent for and came and took supper with him. There followed a long conference, Whitney bluntly pointing out Morgan's low state of finance, credit and reputation, until at last Morgan yielded and consented to accept five hundred dollars and to be taken to Canada; his family meanwhile to be provided for, and in due time sent on to him. They parted on good terms. The plan of his arrest and forcible removal was adopted because of distrust of Morgan's going through with the agreement; and effectually to prevent Miller from knowing of his destination.

From Ft. Niagara, Morgan was taken across the river and the party, by appointment, met two Canadian Masons who were apprised of the plan of settling Morgan somewhere in Canada. They agreed to perform their part if given time to make the necessary arrangements. On Sunday night, September 17, they returned to Ft. Niagara, received Morgan, with him crossed the river and travelled all the rest of that night and the next day on horseback. On Monday night, they reached a point near Hamilton, Ontario, where the journey ended. They paid Morgan the five hundred dollars as agreed and received his signed promise not to return without the permission of either Captain William King, Sheriff Bruce or Whitney. Afterwards, when his disappearance had roused such commotion, Captain King went to Hamilton to bring Morgan back to allay the excitement. But Morgan had disappeared and no trace of him could be found.

There were two other confessions, one by R. H. Hill, who, soon after the disappearance of Morgan, signed a written confession that he had murdered him. He was brought into court, but adjudged insane and discharged. His confession was but the disordered fancy of a diseased mind. Greene published the confession of Henry L. Valance, taken he says from a book of which he could not find a copy. The confession was said to have been made to a physician when Valance was dying. If these confessions were consistent, it would be difficult to ignore them. But they were inconsistent in most important details. In the Weed report of Whitney's confession, five men were named as participating in the drowning of Morgan, but the names of Valance and Hill are not among the five. Valance said there were but three in the party and that he was the one who actually pushed Morgan overboard.

Here then are the two conflicting explanations of the fate of William Morgan; the one, that under pressure, he consented to leave the country and with five hundred dollars in his pocket, deserted his family, yielded to his new sense of freedom, probably shipped in the crew of some vessel at Montreal, travelled from shore to shore until his end came. The other, that he was brutally murdered; his weighted body thrown into the Niagara River: the river and lake, in spite of exhaustive dragging and searching, refusing to yield up their secret. To the end of time, men will differ as to which is the true account. His ultimate fate remains as much a mystery today as it was in 1826.

But Masons of today have no difficulty in drawing the moral line in this episode. Masonry cannot condone either kidnapping or murder or the usurpation of powers of court and Government, by any person or any group of persons or under any provocation. However base the offense, taking its punishment into one's own hand is a violation of law and of human rights, is a policy dangerous to the general welfare, and is to be censured in strongest terms. In the heat of the Anti-Masonic agitation, the Grand Lodge of Masons of Vermont issued an address which represents the true Masonic position. They said:

"We are charged with being accessories to the abduction of William Morgan; with shielding Masons from just judgments for crimes which they have committed; with exercising an influence through Masonic character over the legislative, executive and judicial branches of the Government; with the assumption of a power to judge an individual brother, by a law known only to ourselves; and to inflict corporeal punishment, even unto death.

"To each and every one of the above charges as men whose character is known, and who rely upon the future accountability, we reply in the most solemn manner, that we are guiltless; and that Masonry, so far as we are acquainted with it, in no way or manner, yields its sanction to such principles or practices.

"Masons, above all men, must obey the laws of God and Men. Their solemn obligations require a strict obedience of those laws. So far from binding him to any engagement inconsistent with the happiness, prosperity and welfare of the nation, these obligations doubly require him to be true to his God, his country and his fellowmen. In the language of the ancient Constitution of the Order, which is in print and open to be inspected by all men, he is charged 'to keep and obey the moral law; to be a quiet and peaceable citizen, true to his government and just to his country'."

Masonry acknowledges no laws of its own that contravene the law and constitution that govern all citizens. It claims no right, nor exercises it, to inflict any punishment on its members except suspension or expulsion. It forbids the introduction of political or religious discussion within the lodge. It guarantees to every member entire liberty to worship God as he chooses and to entertain whatever opinions (within the law) seem to him to be right and true.

CHAPTER IV

THE AFTERMATH
WIDESPREAD ATTACK ON MASONRY

THE disappearance of Morgan did not halt his coworker, David C. Miller, in his publication scheme. On the morning of Morgan's arrest at Danold's Tavern, he delivered, at Chesebro's insistence, all of the unprinted manuscripts in his possession. Later, Mrs. Morgan gave to Hiram Ketchum a great bundle of her husband's papers. Daniel Johns, at first Miller's partner and afterward his antagonist in the courts, seized all the printed sheets of the book, that he could lay his hands on. This left Miller with practically nothing of Morgan's version of Masonry to print. But there were numerous treatises in print, notably an English book, "Jachin and Boaz," of which editions appeared in America in 1798, 1803, 1812, 1817 and 1818. Largely from this material, Miller prepared the book which he called, "Illustrations of Freemasonry by William Morgan." On December 15, 1826, Miller's *Batavia Advocate* printed his announcement of the finished work.

Just published
And for sale at The Advocate Office.
The First Part of Masonry Unveiled,
containing a full exposition of the secrets and ceremonies of that 'Ancient and Honorable' Order.
FREE MASONRY
And God Said, *"Let there be light and there was light."*
The remaining part is now in press and will shortly be published.

The much-heralded work, at first, was sold for one dollar per copy. Perhaps the demand was not so great as had been anticipated. At any rate, the price was soon reduced to fifty cents, then to twenty-five, at last to a York shilling, twelve and a half cents. No one, it is believed, made any profits out of the publication. It was immediately pirated in all quarters, and the book has been reprinted by hundreds of thousands from 1827 to the present time.

The original edition was followed by other and greatly enlarged works of the same nature. Rev. David Bernard, a Baptist Minister of LeRoy, N. Y., edited one giving explanation of fifty other Masonic (?) degrees. Avery Allen, an Anti-Masonic lecturer of the period, edited another which was entitled, "Ritual of Freemasonry, illustrated with numerous engravings to which is added a Key to Phi Beta Kappa, The Orange, and Odd Fellows Society," in which still other alleged Masonic degrees were recited.

Meanwhile events were occurring that roused increasing sentiment against the fraternity. On September 10, 1826, Miller's printing office was found afire. The flames were quickly extinguished and little damage was done. Miller immediately charged the Masons with responsibility for the fire and they retorted with an offer of a reward for the detection of the incendiarists, plainly intimating their belief that Miller himself set the fire in order to arouse sympathy for himself and indignation against the Masons.

On September 8, Johns, the Canadian partner of Miller, brought suit against him for recovery of moneys advanced ($40.00). On this complaint Miller was arrested and taken to LeRoy. Johns not appearing, the complaint was dismissed and Miller discharged. But his account of the arrest, published in *The Advocate*, profoundly stirred the County already at fever heat over Morgan's disappearance.

Citizen's meetings, plainly advertised as Anti-Masonic, began to be held. The first was at Batavia on September 25, two weeks after Morgan's arrest, followed by another on October 4. Then came Governor Clinton's first proclamation, October 7. In December the Grand Jury of Ontario County returned indictments against Nicholas G. Chesebro, Loton Lawson, Edward Sawyer and John Sheldon, charging them with conspiracy "to seize and carry William Morgan to foreign parts, and there continually to secrete and imprison him." On January 1, 1827, their trial was begun at Canandaigua.

On January 13, 1827, an Anti-Masonic Convention was held at Seneca, N. Y. It was speedily followed by others at Lewiston, N. Y., and at Canandaigua (January 31). On February 3, Thurlow Weed, who had been employed on a Rochester paper, was given a bonus of four thousand dollars with which to start an Anti-Masonic paper at Albany. During February and March of that year (1827) twelve Anti-Masonic Conventions were held in as many cities of central New York.

In October, the finding of the body of the drowned man, with the contradictory verdicts of the different juries, gave the movement a fresh start. In December, 1827, Captain William King, John Whitney and Burrage Smith were indicted for the murder of Morgan. They had removed from N. Y. State; and their pursuit, financed by an appropriation by the Legislature, was undertaken. Captain King afterwards returned and issued an address to the public maintaining that his removal from the State and from point to point (as he gave in detail) was on orders of the Government; and demanding investigation and trial. But he was one of the few, in any way mentioned in the affair, who was not put on trial.

Churches participated in the general attack on the fraternity by barring Masons from their pulpits and in resolutions condemning the alleged "irreligious" tendencies of the institution. A Baptist Conference at Whitesboro, N. Y., October 22–24, 1829, in which ten counties were represented, adopted these resolutions:—

"Resolved, that in the opinion of this Conference, it is the duty of every member of our churches who is a Free Mason, to dissolve all connection with the Masonic Fraternity, and hold himself no longer bound by any ties of allegiance to the Masonic Institution, or by its obligations, laws, usages or customs; and that he give to his church satisfactory evidence of the same.

"Resolved, that this Conference earnestly recommend to our churches, to practice all Christian forbearance to their Masonic Brethren; but that in case they cannot be induced to take the step above described, it will finally be the duty of churches to withdraw the Hand of Christian Fellowship from these brethren."

A convention which met at Elbo, N. Y., March 3, 1827, adopted a briefer, more pointed resolution, which was typical of those adopted by hundreds of other gatherings and organizations.

"Resolved, that we will not support any person for any office either in town, county or state; nor hear any preacher of the Gospel, who is a member of the Masonic Fraternity."

As indicating the intense excitement aroused by this agitation, the following incident is related. A Summer St. John's Day Celebration had been arranged to be held at Batavia in June, 1827. When the day came, a hostile throng (estimated at 12,000 persons) had gathered. Batavia's population was only 1350. Many favored a postponement of the celebration, but it was decided that they could not afford, as Masons, to appear to be afraid or ashamed. So they quietly and unostentatiously went through with their program. Clothed in white aprons and gloves, they marched slowly to the Church through the dense crowd which opened to let them pass. There were many insulting remarks and a false move would have led to violence. But they held their exercises, listened to a thoughtful address, quietly returned to the lodge room and dispersed.

At the LeRoy convention, June, 1827, resolutions were adopted denouncing the fraternity and giving seventeen reasons for their condemnation.

1. It exercises power over the persons and lives of citizens.
2. It arrogates to itself the right to punish its members for offences unknown to the law of the land.
3. It requires the concealment of crime; and protects the guilty from punishment.

4. It encourages the commission of crime by affording the means of escape.

5. It assumes dignities and titles inconsistent with a republican government.

6. It affords an opportunity for the corrupt and designing to form plans against the government and against individuals.

7. It destroys the principles of equality by bestowing favors on its own members and excluding others equally meritorious.

8. It creates odious aristocracies by obligations to support the interests of members in preference to others of equal qualifications.

9. It blasphemes the name and attempts the personification of Jehovah.

10. It prostitutes the Sacred Scriptures to unholy purposes, to subserve its own secular and trifling forms.

11. It weakens the sentiments of morality and religion by the multiplication of profane oaths and an immoral familiarity with religious forms and ceremonies.

12. It encourages in its ceremonies an unholy commingling of divine truth with impious human inventions.

13. It substitutes selfrighteousness and the ceremonies of Freemasonry for vital religion and the ordinances of the Gospel.

14. It promotes habits of idleness and intemperance by the members neglecting business to attend meetings and to drink libations.

15. It accumulates funds at the expense of the indigent and to the damage of females; and dissipates them in rioting and pleasure and its own senseless ceremonies and exhibitions.

16. It contracts the sympathies of human hearts from all the unfortunate by confining charities to its own members.

17. It destroys veneration for religion and religious ordinances by the profane use of religious forms.

Thurlow Weed in his *Albany Journal*, Solomon Southwick in his *Rochester Observer*, and Henry Ward Dana's *Anti-Masonic Review* in New York City, gave repeated publication to these attacks. The opposition spread to other States. In Pennsylvania there were large groups who had been conscientiously opposed to the taking of any oaths:—The Quakers, the Lutherans, the many German sects such as the Mennonites, the Dunkards, the Moravians, the Schwenkfelders and the German Reformed Churches. All these were naturally prejudiced against the fraternity and were easily aroused to active opposition.

In New England, Masonry had been very strong in numbers and in influence. Her heroes and leaders of Revolutionary Days were members and sponsors of the Craft. At the same time, throughout New England there was a general orthodoxy and a Puritanical devotion to evangelical religion that made it extremely sensitive to the charge that Masonry was inimical to religion. In Vermont, the Legislature passed an Act forbidding extrajudicial oaths. Masons were deprived of local offices, stricken from jury rolls, injured in business, wounded in their domestic relations, and in many instances, driven to emigration. Gould, in his *History of Freemasonry*, has this to say of the spirit of those days:—

"This country has seen fierce and bitter political contests; but no other has approached the bitterness of this campaign against the Masons. No society, civil, military or religious escaped its influence. No relation of family or friends was a barrier to it. The hatred of Masonry was carried everywhere, and there was no retreat so sacred that it did not enter. Not only were teachers and pastors driven from their stations, but the children of Masons were excluded from the schools, and members from their churches. The Sacrament was refused to Masons by formal vote of the church, for no other offense than their Masonic connection. Families were divided. Brother was arrayed against brother, father against son, and even wives against their husbands. Desperate efforts were made to take away chartered rights from Masonic Corporations and to pass laws that would prevent Masons from holding their meetings and performing their ceremonies."

It is not to be supposed that Masons made no defense to these bitter attacks. Lodges and Grand Lodges took action disavowing any knowledge of the Morgan abduction; condemning it as an offense obnoxious alike to the principles of Masonry, to the laws of the country and to the laws of God and asserting their devotion to religion, morality, liberty and good government. They repeatedly declared that Masonry inculcated no principle, and authorized no acts not in perfect harmony with true religion, good morals, civil liberty and lawful government.

The nine lodges of Monroe County, New York, united in surrendering their charters in acquiescence with public opinion. But in their address explaining their action, they said, "Let it not be supposed that we mean to admit that there is anything in Masonry, as we have severally received and practised it, immoral in its tendency, in any wise dangerous to civil or religious liberty, or opposed to the Christian Religion."

But the pressure was so strong that withdrawals by individuals and bodies were numerous. In 1827, two hundred and twenty-seven lodges were represented in the Grand Lodge of New York. In 1835, the number had dwindled to forty-one. Every lodge in the State of Vermont surrendered its charter or became dormant; and the Grand Lodge, for several years, ceased to hold its sessions. As in Vermont, so also in Pennsylvania, Rhode Island, Massachusetts, Connecticut; and in lesser degree in several other states. The Masonic Temple was cleft in twain; its brotherhood scattered; its trestle board without work; its working tools shattered. Thus Masonry endured the penalty of the mistaken zeal of those fearful brethren who thought that the revealing of the ritual to profane eyes would destroy the Order and who hoped to save it by removing the traitor within the camp.

CHAPTER V

The Anti-Masonic Party

AMERICAN historians have usually treated the Anti-Masonic Party as the natural and immediate outgrowth of the nation-wide resentment against Masons for their treatment of William Morgan. A moment's reflection, however, must convince one that a movement so widespread and sustained by so many of the greatest political leaders of the period, must have had broader underlying causes. The Morgan incident was the spark that set off the powder magazine. It was no more the effective cause of the movement, than was the "Diamond Necklace" incident, which involved Marie Antoinette, the cause of the French Revolution and the ending of the dynasty of the Bourbons; or, the assassination of the Crown Prince of Austria by the young Servian student at Sarajevo the cause of the World War. In each instance forces, many and involved, social, racial, religious and political, had been working beneath the surface and needed only some incident that would fire the passions of men, to bring the conflict out into the open.

Anti-Masonry was but one of many confluent streams that made up the current of thought and passion that swept through the nation in that decade, 1825–1835. Some might say, not very important. Woodrow Wilson does not even mention the movement in his History of the American People. Yet while it lasted, the movement was served by its advocates with a spirit almost of frenzy. Like any movement that seems to attack the personal, individual liberties of citizens, it aroused intense passion. A review of the growth of political parties in America up to this period, reveals conditions ripe for political strife and for the launching of a new party.

Washington was a national figure, not a party man. His service in the War of the Revolution, his steadying influence in the formation of the new government, had been so unique, his personality so dominant, that his elections to the Presidency were by unanimous vote of the Electoral College. Yet even in the Constitutional Convention (convened at Philadelphia, May 14, 1787) sharp divisions appeared as parties in embryo. The debate was chiefly on two points—the general government to coerce the States, and the question of representation in Congress, whether it should be by States or in proportion to population. One group would give to Congress unquestioned supremacy; the other would refer all power directly to the people, and maintain the independence of the States.

The convention secured an agreement of its members by adopting a compromise which gave the States equal representation in the Senate; and representation in the House proportionate to population. Out of this debate grew the names of the first national political parties, Federal and Anti-Federal. The former maintained the paramount need of a strong central government; the latter would have limited the powers of that central government by very definite restrictions and by clear definition of State rights. Alexander Hamilton and John Adams were the chief defenders of the theory of the strong central government; while Jefferson, Madison and Randolph were their chief opponents. Washington, half-gracious, half-austere, wholly commanding, maintained a lofty supremacy to party, but in actual practice as President pursued the policies of the Federalists.

Of course, he was not able to avoid divisions of sentiment among the people. During his first administration, a serious crisis developed when it was proposed that the National Government assume the war debts of the individual colonies (now States). Representatives of the Southern States were solidly against the measure until Hamilton, by his astute leadership, won the votes necessary to carry the measure. The South had been very desirous that the new Capital of the Nation should be fixed along the shores of the Potomac. This would be within their easy reach and somewhat removed from the dominant influence of the three great Northern cities, Boston, New York and Philadelphia, and from New England with its frequent and troublesome suggestion of the abolishment of slavery. Hamilton arranged that his measure for the assumption of the war debts and this bill for the locating of the Capital on the border of Virginia, should be brought up for joint action in Congress. The result was that the South yielded on the one point to gain the other and so the storm cleared away.

An even sharper crisis developed in Washington's second administration. It was concerned with the relations of America with foreign nations. It was 1793, the year when revolution swept France with terror. The Monarchy was abolished. Louis XVI and his queen were beheaded. The Republic was set up in France, fashioned somewhat like our own and with all Europe arrayed against it. No one over there doubted that America would join hands with France in this struggle against tyranny. Citizen Genet, first Minister to America from the French Republic, landed at Charleston, South Carolina, from a French frigate and his journey to Philadelphia was like a triumphal procession. He confidently assumed America as the ally of his Government and on that assumption, even before presenting his credentials to President Washington, had commissioned privateers to prey on British commerce and directed French ships to bring their prizes into American ports where French Consuls would conduct prize courts for their confiscation. Jefferson loved France with whose watchwords, "Liberty, Equality and Fraternity," he so strongly sympathized. He welcomed Genet as a warm personal friend. The two nations had been linked in close alliance in our War of the Revolution and Jefferson interpreted our pledges of mutual assistance then given, as applicable to France in her struggles with all Europe.

But Washington, unperturbed by the current of enthusiasm for France that was sweeping the country, quietly, sternly held to his principle of justice and right in our dealings with all countries, of neutrality, of freedom from complications and entangling alliances in European affairs. Genet was soon superseded. The Cabinet supported Washington in the crisis. Jefferson himself, as Secretary of State, drew and signed the Proclamation of Neutrality which the President insisted must be issued.

But feeling continued to run high in the country. There were banquets in all cities, celebrating the rights of man. Democratic Clubs, modeled after the Jacobin Club of Paris, were formed in great numbers and these became the nuclei of a party now taking definite form which would contest with the Federalists for the control of the Government. In December, 1793, Jefferson withdrew from the Cabinet to be free to lead the party to its triumph, after Washington had retired from the stage of affairs.

The influence of Washington was too strong, however, in the first contest, and with his support John Adams was chosen second President of the United States. But in that campaign of 1796, the antagonism grew very bitter and the election was very close. Pinckney of South Carolina had been put forward by the Federalists with Adams; with the intent that Adams should be President and Pinckney, Vice-President. There was no provision, as now, for the naming of Electors for President and Vice-President separately. Two candidates were named by each party and the Electors chosen could determine the ranking. Difficulties of communication made it impossible for Electors of distant States to communicate with each other during the period between their election and the time for the actual casting of the vote of the Electoral College. The North was suspicious of the South; and the South was jealous of New England. In the fear that the Federalist Electors of the South might cast their votes for Pinckney for President (rather than for Adams), several of the Northern States that had been carried by the Federalists, cast their votes for others than Pinckney. In the South, hoping to have the Government entirely in Southern hands, South Carolina, regardless of party ties, cast her vote for Jefferson and Pinckney. The result was the choice of Adams, the Federalist, for President; and Jefferson, the Republican-Democrat, for Vice-President.

Adams is pictured as a man easily stung by jealousies, sensitive to criticism, irascible, hasty, intolerant; a man to be trusted in the long run and to stand loyal and steady to sound convictions; but not a man to love or to be regarded above party.

The same difficulties over foreign relations that had darkened Washington's second administration, continued to harass Adams, the people who were interested in commerce demanding war with England for her continual unfriendly acts. Others insisted on war with France, now under the Directorate, for even more outrageous methods. Adams retained the Cabinet of Washington (all Federalists); but as time went on, they were more and more inclined to look to Hamilton rather than Adams, as the real leader of their party.

In anger, Adams at last dismissed his Cabinet in a body and broke completely with Hamilton, to the demoralization of the Federal Party. At the end of his term, the Federalists again named Adams and Pinckney, the Republican-Democrats offering Jefferson and Aaron Burr. The turning of New York against Adams cost him re-election. In the Electoral College, the Democrats remembering the experience of the Federalists in 1796 and fearing to begin dividing their ballots to express preference between Jefferson and Burr, voted solidly for both. Much to Jefferson's chagrin, this vote automatically threw the election into the House. There the Federalists had the balance of power and were called on to decide which of the Democratic candidates they preferred. A long and bitter contest followed. The vote stood unchanged for 35 ballots; eight States voting for Jefferson, six for Burr and two divided. Hamilton used all his influence to swing the vote to Jefferson and finally succeeded.

With this critical election the Federal Party lost its control of the Government and never regained it. In his inaugural address Jefferson made a plea that the Government be a Government of the whole people rather than a party. "We are all Republican—we are all Federalist," is a phrase that became proverbial during the "era of good feeling." "We are not antagonists," he pleaded, "but live by an absolute acquiescence in the decisions of the majority—the vital principle of a Republic. Let us unite with one mind, let us restore to social intercourse that harmony and affection without which liberty and life itself are dreary things."

In all this Jefferson voiced the spirit of his day. It was impossible that the conservative ruling classes of the older day should continue to govern the young nation that was springing into life. The great spaces of virgin land in the West were filling and there stirred everywhere the air of enterprise and change. Democracy, an equal footing for all men in opinion, effort and attainment, were the very conditions of its being.

But it was easier to plead for harmony that to attain it. The Old World was in constant and desperate conflict. Napoleon needed the supplies and resources of the young Republic of the West and was willing to pay richly for them. This meant riches untold for American merchants and shipowners. Great Britain must prevent this commerce to ports in all lands under Bonaparte's control or confess him unconquerable. Jefferson determinedly kept peace. As alternative to war, he forced through the Embargo Act, forbidding all commerce. The closing year of his Presidency was darkened and distressed by its effects. Ships rotted at the wharves; quays were deserted; Southern planters and New England merchants were in equal distress. At last Jefferson yielded. Almost his last official act was the signing of a bill that permitted trade with all the world, except with France and Great Britain. Then with a sigh of relief, he turned the government over to Madison, leaving him to face the two unfriendly Powers.

It is evidence of the complete collapse of any opposition party that under such circumstances, Jefferson was able to name his successor; and again eight years afterwards, to name as the nominee, James Monroe, fourth Virginian to be elevated to the Presidency. When Monroe's first term had expired, it seemed that Jefferson's statement, "We are all Republicans, we are all Federalists," was literally true. For when the Electors met in their several states, only one Elector, (from New Hampshire) indulged himself in an individual choice. He voted for John Quincy Adams; all other votes were for Monroe.

The disappearance of the Federalist Party, however, did not mean the obliteration of the old divisions and the old antagonisms. New figures were coming into leadership in national life; and if there was but one nation there were many factions. They were grouped now, not around policies and traditions, but about the personal standards of these new leaders. In 1824 there was a veritable scramble for the Presidency. It showed how deceptive had been the political calm of the past years—that "Era of Good Feeling."

Henry Clay came into immediate prominence on his entrance to the House. He was not yet thirty-five years of age; had an easy way comradeship with men and a ready mastery in debate which gave him an engaging prominence. His free pose, his candid utterance, his dash and telling vigor bespoke him the man of the new and confident West. He was chosen Speaker of the House, and became its acknowledged leader. Now the legislatures of five States put him forward as their candidate.

General Andrew Jackson caught the imagination of the country by his spectacular victory at New Orleans and his high-handed conquest of Florida. The old Democratic party-caucus, which had dominated nomination through six successive Presidential campaigns, put forward Crawford of Georgia who had been Monroe's Secretary of the Treasury. But it was generally understood that John Quincy Adams of Massachusetts, a former Federalist, Monroe's Secretary of State was the real choice of the old leaders. To the surprise of most of the leaders, General Jackson led in the ballot in the Electoral College, the vote standing: Jackson, 99 votes; Adams, 84; Crawford, 41; and Henry Clay, 37. There being no majority the election was thrown into the House, the second in the history of the Republic. In the House, Clay threw his force to Adams. There were bitter charges of the purchase of the Presidency, when, immediately afterwards, Adams appointed Clay Secretary of State. And there was a general feeling that the defeat of Jackson with his plurality of votes was a violation of the will of the majority; and the choice of Adams a turning back to the old order which would be corrected at the earliest possible moment.

Jackson loomed up as the dominant figure who would hereafter, for his time, control the Democratic party and the National Government. His sturdy independence, his disregard of conventional courtesies, his rugged defiance of opposition, his fearless courage, his violent overriding of antagonists, were elements that made him many enemies. Besides, there were many other disaffected groups, quite apart from these personal foes of Jackson. The liberal Democracy of Jefferson had never obtained any firm foothold in New England nor among the more conservative class in some other States. It was inevitable in a party so long continued in power, that there should be many malcontents. Some had profited greatly in honor and in pocket; but the many had no direct reward for their loyal support. The West, the South, the East all had their special interests and each its different social ideals. All these differences were intensified by the social upheaval of this remarkable period.

CHAPTER VI

Conditions in New York State.

IN the State of New York, especially, matters politically were awry. Much of the struggle concerning the Constitution had centered about Alexander Hamilton. That great leader of the Federalists had been cut down. The party in the State felt his loss keenly. The Erie Canal had been a constant source of contention in the politics of the State. DeWitt Clinton championed its construction and operation. The Bucktails (originally a name applied to a faction within Tammany Hall, afterward applied to the party in the State opposed to Clinton's Erie Canal leadership) led by Martin Van Buren, as vigorously opposed it. In 1826 Clinton joined forces politically with Van Buren, thus leaving the friends of the Canal leaderless and disorganized. New York was just in the mood to be attracted to some issue that was new, direct, with a question of morals involved in it, that made its appeal to the consciences and prejudices of men.

Yet no one could have supposed that an incident so local, so personal as the Morgan abduction could have been the agency to make men forget their differences and their old antagonisms and fuse them into a sturdy political party. To make anything of this movement politically needed skilful guidance and canny fostering. It happened that there were brilliant leaders at hand—youthful, resourceful, ambitious, unattached, adrift from the old parties, reaching out for something new. This Anti-Masonic party could not hold them long; it was too limited in its scope for that. But it was the bridge that carried over until the Whig party indicated its strength and they went over into it.

The first of these leaders was Thurlow Weed; a Journalist and political leader who for more than fifty years wielded a potent influence in the politics of his State and Nation. He was born at Cairo, Greene County, New York, November 15, 1797. At fourteen he was apprenticed as a printer and served as such until the outbreak of the War of 1812 in which he served as a volunteer on the Northern frontier. After the war he engaged in several journalistic adventures, until he became Editor of the *Rochester Telegraph* in 1822. He took active and belligerent part in the Morgan case from the very start. When his activities in the matter seemed to bring injury to his paper he withdrew, and very shortly was given a bonus to start an Anti-Masonic paper which was called the *Anti-Masonic Enquirer*. He served two terms in the State Legislature where he was noted for his remarkable adroitness as a political manager. In 1830 he founded the *Albany Evening Journal*, an Anti-Jackson organ which he edited with remarkable ability for thirty-three years.

It was said that his influence in political affairs, first as an Anti-Mason, afterward as a Whig, and still later as a Republican, was in some respects unsurpassed by that of any other man in public life. Declining office for himself, except the profitable one of State Printer, he dictated the nomination and appointment of others. To his skilful management was credited the nominations of Harrison in 1840 and Taylor in 1848, while he took a leading part in the nominations of Clay in 1844, Scott in 1852 and Fremont in 1856. Throughout his long career, he was the intimate friend of William H. Seward and for a long time was an influential member of the powerful political firm of Seward, Weed and Greely. He seemed early to sense the transient nature of the Anti-Masonic Party, for in just a few years he turned his energies in other directions. But in its early years, he was unquestionably its most forceful worker. He personally visited every one with any knowledge of the case; he called the citizens of Batavia together; he pressed the matter in the court; he urged action in the Legislature. He followed up those concerned, gathered witnesses against them and in his papers tirelessly kept the matter before the public. Through extensive correspondence, by constant visitation, by careful planning of the details of the many citizens' meetings and conventions, he kept the matter alive and made it an issue that could not be ignored.

He never lost his interest in the Morgan case. In his Autobiography, he deals with it in great fullness. To the end of his life he resented, very feelingly, the charge that he had disfigured the body of the drowned man to make it coincide with the description of Morgan and especially the charge of O'Reilly, a rival Editor in Rochester. O'Reilly's story was, that at the third inquest over the body of the drowned man when the

Coroner's Jury brought in its verdict that the body was that of Munroe and not of Morgan, he said to Weed, "What will you do for a Morgan now?" and that Weed replied, "I guess this is a good enough Morgan until after election." Weed insisted that what he really said was, "I guess this is a good enough Morgan until Morgan himself is found." But "Good enough Morgan" was a taunt that was thrown at him until the end of his life.

The second great leader of the party in New York was Rev. Dr. Charles C. Finney, the great Evangelist, preacher and College President. He was born at Warren, Connecticut (1792). While a student of law, he was admitted to a Connecticut Lodge of Masons. Through a remarkable religious experience, he was converted and became a very active Christian propagandist. He gave up the law, studied theology and was ordained as a Presbyterian Minister. From 1824 to 1835 (the full period of the Morgan and Anti-Masonic excitement) he traveled from town to town through all Central and Western New York as an itinerant Evangelist. His revivals were marked with unusual manifestations of spiritual power and he exercised a profound influence on every community in which he labored. He was keenly conscientious and after his conversion became convinced that he had been in error in becoming a Mason. His scruples grew in their hold upon him until he felt obliged not merely to withdraw from the Order, but to speak and write against it. He was largely instrumental in influencing churches and communities to ally themselves in vigorous opposition to the Order.

There were others who attained even higher national fame. William H. Seward, Lincoln's Secretary of State, in 1828–1832 was a rising young politician in the legislature with Weed. He lent his great gifts of tongue and pen in the attack on Masonry. Millard Fillmore, who was later to attain the Presidency, was another of the Anti-Masonic group in the Legislature at this time. He was keenly interested in the contest over the Erie Canal and took active part in the legislative support of the prosecution of the Morgan abductors and in organizing the movement as a political force.

There were others of lesser fame, who in a movement of this limited scope, could become active leaders and workers; Solomon Southwick, Editor and Lecturer, who was to be the first Anti-Masonic candidate for Governor of the State; Francis Grainger, another member of the Legislature, and William H. Maynard, elected State Senator from the Fifth District and said to be one of the most gifted men of the party.

Naturally the first activities of the party were concerned with local politics in the towns of central New York. The town meetings furnished the forums where the sentiment was manufactured. Their resolution to withdraw all political support from Masons brought the issue squarely before the voters. From the petty politics of the towns to the higher politics of the State Government, the Masonic proscription speedily spread.

Though Adams had the Presidency, his party was dwindling to the vanishing point in Western New York and those who were opposed to Jackson turned to the new Party as affording the only effective opposition. On the other hand many Masons who had been hostile to Jackson, turned to his support rather than be allied with the hated Anti-Masonic Party.

The first State Election in which the new Party was engaged was in November, 1827. A new Legislature was to be elected and candidates were nominated on the Anti-Masonic platform in all the region affected by the Morgan excitement. Their success in the election astonished even the Anti-Masons themselves, and opened the eyes of the politicians to the fact that the new party was a force to be reckoned with. They elected their candidate in seven of the counties: Chautauqua, Monroe, Otsego, Orleans, Seneca, Wayne and Yates, and now had a compact block of fifteen members in the lower house of the State Legislature.

An amusing incident occurred in the Eighth Senatorial District, which was the very hotbed of their cause. In their haste they had nominated an influential man of the District, only to discover when the campaign was on, that he was a Mason. They switched their votes on election day to the nominee of the "Blacktail" party and he was elected by a large majority. In the legislature they now outnumbered the Adams party which had but twelve members and superseded it as the second party in the State.

This evidence of the growth of the movement so

alarmed the Jackson leaders who feared its effect on the approaching Presidential election that they took steps to conciliate the Anti-Masons and to divert the movement from its antagonism to Jackson. In the Legislature of 1827, Francis Grainger, for the Morgan Zealots, introduced a resolution authorizing a Commission to investigate the affair. The debate on the resolution was exceedingly bitter and it was defeated by a vote of nearly three to one. This seeming determination to repress investigation only served to arouse a more heated purpose to accomplish it. Yielding to this clamor, the Jackson leaders, in an effort to conciliate the Anti-Masons, now introduced and helped to pass in substance the very bill they had defeated less than a year before.

But Jackson was a Mason, Grand Master of Masons of his State. Adams was not and in a letter which was widely published during the campaign, he declared, "I am not a Mason; I never have been; and I never will be." It soon became apparent that the Anti-Masonic forces were in active alliance with the Adams party. As that situation became increasingly clear, the Jackson speakers began to attack the coalition on the high ground of public policy. They charged that the friends of the Administration were using the tense feeling throughout New York State concerning Morgan's fate, to further interests of President Adams and were sparing no pains to contribute to the public agitation with that end in view.

There were Masons, too, in the Adams party and they

took offense at this alliance with their foes and openly resented it. An extract from the *Albany Daily Advertiser* (April 5, 1828) which was strongly supporting Adams, expressed their resentment.

"Their persecuting and unhallowed principle has extended itself to the Presidential contest, and the most disgraceful measures are now taken to make the Masonic question bear on that important election. It is said that one of the candidates for that high office is a Mason, and therefore he must be opposed: that his opponent is not one, and therefore he must be supported. To this course we offer our strong and solemn protest. We know not whether Mr. Adams is a Mason and we care not. We are in favor of his re-election but we must forever despise ourselves did we desire to gain a single vote through the Anti-Masonic excitement; and we look with contempt, almost with horror, on those who endeavor to further his election by such means."

Weed, who had become the Adams leader in the State, was assiduous in his efforts to make the alliance more effective. Campaign funds were used to finance local papers that would make prominent the Morgan story and play on the prejudices already aroused to fever heat. He furthered the holding of frequent Anti-Masonic conventions in different cities and succeeded in winning over some of the brightest men of the State who were opposed to Jackson and were convinced that the Adams party was in the hands of men not able to steer it to a successful issue. Thus he tried to make capital for Adams out of both the Anti-Jackson and Anti-Masonic sentiments.

When the Anti-Masonic State Convention was held at LeRoy, N. Y., on July 4, 1828, Weed persuaded it to make no nomination for Governor; but to wait until the Adams party convention met at Utica July 23 and to endorse its candidate, if acceptable. Some of the shrewder and more single minded Anti-Masons began to suspect that they were being used by the politicians. At the LeRoy convention the following resolution was adopted.

"*Resolved,* Whatever may be our predilections for the candidates now before the public for the Presidency, and whatever part we as individuals may see fit to take in the national politics, we consider the same as entirely disconnected with Anti-Masonry, and of vastly paramount importance. That the Convention would view with undissembled feelings of regret, any attempt to render the honest indignation now existing against the Masonic institution subservient to the views of any of the political parties of the day; that we do most unhesitatingly disclaim all intentions of promoting political principles."

The Utica convention nominated Judge Smith Thompson for Governor and Francis Grainger for Lieutenant Governor. Thompson was not a Mason but had taken no part in the Anti-Masonic movement. Grainger was a zealous Anti-Mason and had been active in the legislature in the interests of the Morgan investigation. Weed, in his autobiography, gives an account of the convention and explains that the rural delegates preferred Grainger as the nominee for governor, but it was deemed wiser to name Thompson in as much as the naming of Grainger avowedly to catch the Anti-Masonic vote would have alienated so many national Republicans as to jeopardize the presidential ticket.

The extreme Anti-Masons were not to be reconciled, however, and called a second convention to meet

August 4 at LeRoy. Its delegates voted "to disregard the two great parties, that at this time distract the State and the Union, in the choice of candidates for office; and to proceed at once to the nomination of the Anti-Masonic candidates." They then placed in nomination, Francis Grainger for Governor and John Grary, of Washington County, for Lieutenant Governor. His nomination for two different offices by two different parties placed Grainger in a very difficult position. He cut the Gordian knot by issuing his acceptance of the nomination for Lieutenant Governor on the Adams ticket. Though greatly chagrined, the more radical Anti-Masons were not to be easily deprived of their own candidate. They held still a third convention at LeRoy September 7 and nominated Solomon Southwick of whose extreme and persistent Anti-Masonry there was no question. Southwick had been a Mason but was now most violent in his denunciation of the fraternity. During the whole period of the Morgan excitement, he continued its most picturesque if sometimes ludicrous figure. He had a fog-horn voice and his campaign was at least noisy and vociferous.

The election in November showed the following result:

Democratic	Martin Van Buren	136,794
Whig	Smith Thompson	106.444
Anti-Masonic	Solomon Southwick	33,345

In the legislature, the Anti-Masons slightly increased their strength. In the Assembly they had a representation of seventeen members, and in the Senate succeeded in carrying four Districts, where in the year before they had none. The same counties that showed Anti-Masonic strength on the State ticket gave Adams his best support. However eighteen electors were chosen who were favorable to Jackson and sixteen in favor of Adams.

Thurlow Weed had been unable to control his extremists of the party and in *The Argus* he announced his withdrawal of support of the ticket. This brought down on his head charges of treason to the cause. Here was the difficulty, which constantly faced the practical leaders of the movement. It was impossible to get harmony between the extremists whose one aim was the extinction of Masonry, and the practical politicians who hoped to build up the party to the point where it could carry elections in its own strength or in alliance with another. It was a chastened Weed, smarting under the criticisms of former associates and perplexed with the difficulty of steering a middle course, who gives this picture of the tense lines of those days:

"The conflict became more embittered and relentless, personally, politically, socially and ecclesiastically than any other I have ever participated in, and more so, probably, than any ever known in this country. The feelings of Masons, exasperated by the existence of a political organization which made war on the institution of Freemasonry, became intensely so by the renunciation of Masonry by Ministers, Elders, Deacons of the Presbyterian, Methodist and Baptist churches. Thousands of Masons, innocent of any wrong doing and intending to remain neutral, were drawn into the conflict, when all were denounced who adhered to the institution."

In the local elections of 1829, there was some further

progress. The party increased its strength in the Assembly to twenty-two members and added one more Senator to its list. The difference in the party had been somewhat healed; Weed was again acknowledged as leader. A convention was held in February, 1829, at Rochester, at which the jarring elements of the party were brought together. McCarty, in his history of the movement, says that this convention marked a new starting point in the life of the party in New York. Bancroft says, "Henceforth, until the Anti-Masonic decline set in, they carried on the most effective system of political propagandism that the State had ever known." The convention issued a call for a national convention to be held in Philadelphia in September, 1830. This indicated that the leaders were ambitious to carry the movement into the broader field of national politics. More and more the movement was directly Anti-Jackson, gathering into itself the remnant of the old Federal party and uniting with it all the elements of discontent that could be rallied to its standard. It was really the beginning of the Whig party.

In the legislature, the Anti-Masonic members acted with a good deal of wisdom and shrewdness. They consistently stood as the advocates of a policy of internal improvements; voting to sustain the maintenance and extension of the Erie Canal and against any raising of the tolls; also the Chenango Canal which would connect the Erie Canal with the Pennsylvania system of waterways through the Susquehanna River. The southern counties of the State were deeply interested in this project and were most favorably attracted to the Anti-Masonic Party by the position taken by its representatives in the legislature. They did not fail to keep up a running attack on Masonry. Trials and investigations went on as before. A memorial was presented to the legislature charging the Grand Lodge with furnishing funds to help the Morgan conspirators. Mr. Spencer, the special prosecutor in the Morgan cases, asked the new Governor Throop for authority to use the fund which Governor Clinton had offered as a reward ($2,000). Throop denied the request and Spencer resigned, charging that the Governor in many ways had failed to support him in his task as prosecutor and had divulged official and confidential communications which had seriously interfered with his securing evidence of Morgan's murder and the detection of the murderers. All this served to keep the matter before the public and strengthened the Anti-Masonic spirit as election again drew near.

The party leaders spared nothing that could be used to strengthen the machinery of its organization. In order to gain voting strength in New York City, it was decided by the leaders to name on the ticket some one from the city who would be representative of the new Workingman's Party. In the convention Mr. Seward was given the task of making the speech which should win the consent of the strict Anti-Masons to this scheme. With wonderful acuteness, he so worded his attack on Masonry as to connect it with all the political events of the year. This passage of his address is quoted from Bancroft:

"In the events which called our party into existence we have proof that the society of Freemasons has broken the public peace; in the guarded and studious silence of the press throughout the Union on the subject of that outrage, we have proof that Masonry has subsidized the press; in the refusal of the Assembly to institute legislative inquiry into the acts of the Masons in relation to that outrage, we have proof that the legislative department has been corrupted; by the withholding by the Governor of all positive aid in bringing to justice the actors in that profligate conspiracy, we have proof that Freemasonry has made a timid executive subservient to its will; and in the escape of the guilty conspirators by means of the Masonic oblitions of witnesses and jurors, we have fearful proof that Masonry has obstructed, defeated, and baffled the judiciary in the high exercise of its powers."

Surely if all this were true, his conclusion is irresistible, "The society of Freemasons ought to be abolished." Even after such an address it was not without difficulty that consent to the scheme was obtained from the strict Anti-Masons. But eventually Grainger was nominated for Governor and Samuel Stevens, a young Alderman of New York City, allied with the Workingman's Party, was named for Lieutenant Governor.

Southwick, who had now been discarded from leadership, turned bitterly upon Weed and Seward and Mr. Grary (former candidate for Lieutenant Governor), declared that the party had lost its integrity and urged all loyal Anti-Masons "to throw off the bondage to men who have entered the party to use it for their own unworthy purposes." But the new leadership was vigorous and bold and enthusiastic and in this campaign was to carry the party to its high water mark in New York State. While defeated, Grainger received 120,361 votes; Throop, the Democratic nominee, was elected with a vote of 128,-892. The nomination of Stevens had failed to change the situation in New York City; and the strongly Masonic counties of Eastern New York voted the Jacksonian rather than the hated Anti-Masonic ticket. The party increased its strength in the Assembly to 33 members out of a total of one hundred and twenty-four. They also slightly increased their strength in the State Senate.

In this Assembly was a group of men that would have honored any party; the eloquent Maynard; Albert Tracy, described as cultured, brilliant and diplomatic; Millard Fillmore, later President of the United States; Francis Grainger, a splendid campaigner and expert legislator; and ablest of all in native ability, William H. Seward who for thirty years was to be recognized as New York's most influential statesman. He was twice Governor of his State, and United States Senator for two terms: in 1860 he just missed the Presidential nomination; then served with distinction as Secretary of State in Lincoln's Cabinet.

Under the leadership of such men, the party made a record in the legislature that won the respect and approval of the people throughout the State. They supported an amendment which changed the militia system to a voluntary service. The militia service had grown so obnoxious that it was said every young man sought to escape its duties. Seward's amendment, therefore, was in great favor. They successfully supported a bill abolishing imprisonment for debt, retaining the penalty only in cases of fraud on the part of the debtor; but forever prohibiting the incarceration of debtors who though unfortunate, were not guilty of dishonesty. They continued active in the interest of the Canal system of the State and other internal improvements. They supported by their arguments and their votes the chartering of the National Bank. This action was opposed by the whole power of the State banks and the debate excited wide and intense interest among the people.

Thus in all these legislative activities the party gave sign of able and vigorous leadership; yet was growing all the while less distinctly Anti-Masonic and becoming more and more a general political body. Its strength and popularity depended on its broader program of service. As to its distinctive issue of Anti-Masonry, it had been pretty clearly demonstrated that this was too narrow and ill-founded a basis on which to build an enduring and successful party.

CHAPTER VII

ANTI-MASONRY IN PENNSYLVANIA

THE story of the Morgan outrage was carried in person and by the Press to the neighboring State of Pennsylvania. In 1827, Whittelsy carried on an active propaganda, sending into the State a continuous stream of Anti-Masonic documents and papers. By 1828, Thurlow Weed's paper (*The Anti-Masonic Enquirer*, published at Rochester) was in circulation in Allegheny, Somerset, Union, Lancaster and Chester counties. The population of Pennsylvania, racially and religiously, was such as to make it likely to lend a responsive ear to the agitation against Masonry. The tier of counties on the northern border was filled with settlers from New England, coming over the border from New York. About Philadelphia, from the earliest settlement of the colony, the Quakers with their quiet, peace-loving, upright thrift and industry were the dominant sect. Penn's policy of fair dealing and religious toleration and universal suffrage had attracted a high type of colonist. Great numbers of Scotch-Irish settled in the valleys along the Susquehanna and farther west of the mountains, while large colonies of Germans from the Palatinate peopled the central and eastern counties.

Every one of these distinctive elements of the population, the Quakers, the New England descendants of the Puritans, the Scotch-Irish, Presbyterians, the numerous German sects, while utterly diverse in many respects, were alike in this: that all had native prejudices and inherited traditions to which the Anti-Masonic agitation made sympathetic and effective appeal. In the church creeds of most of the German sects there were provisions against the taking of any oaths. The Scotch-Irish Presbyterians, through long years of persecution overseas by Catholics and British Prelatists, had come to cherish a firm devotion to their church and their religion, that left no place in their thinking for any institution which, like Masonry, had its ritual and ceremonies so largely fashioned by Biblical verbiage and history. The Quakers had an inherited traditional conviction against an organized church or fixed form of worship; and gloried in their spiritual freedom. They would then have a natural antipathy to the obligations and ritualistic ceremonies of Freemasonry. When to all this natural indifference and hostility to the Order, there was brought the story of the attack on the liberty and life of Morgan, of Masonic juries that would not convict brethren because of Masonic obligation, of courts that were corrupted and legislative bodies controlled by this same alleged malign influence, it is little wonder that a State with such elements in its population should press the attack against the fraternity even more vigorously than New York itself.

The first appearance of Anti-Masonic political activity was in the fall of 1828. William Heister of Lancaster County was nominated for Congress but his party made ineffective opposition to the Democrats in Somerset, Westmoreland and India counties, failing to elect any representative of the party, either to Congress or the State Legislature. But 1829 was the year for the Gubernatorial election and on June 25 of that year, a convention met at Harrisburg with delegates present from ten of the fifty-two counties of the State. Frederick Whittelsey, member of the central committee of Rochester, N. Y., addressed the convention, making a long and bitter attack on Masonry and urged the nomination of a State ticket and the organization of the party for state-wide activity. The convention nominated Joseph Ritner for Governor, a man of German parentage, a soldier of the War of 1812 and a former Speaker of the Lower House of the State Legislature. The Democrats had chosen a Mason as their candidate, George Wolf, who had served three terms in Congress. In spite of ineffective organization, Ritner polled 49,000 votes and actually carried 17 of the 52 counties of the State. The Anti-Masons elected one Congressman (from the Pittsburg District), one State Senator and 15 Assemblymen. The leaders were greatly elated by these partial successes. Indeed the sudden rise of the Party to such strength can only be explained by the fact that the natural elements to attach men to such a movement were all there, waiting to welcome the issue as soon as it would be earnestly presented. The result of the election clearly showed that the people of Pennsylvania were ready for Anti-Masonry and every indication pointed to greater successes as the reward of careful, energetic organization.

The wide diversity of interests before the legislature in that first year of Anti-Masonic representation in Pennsylvania made it almost impossible to hold members in the Assembly to any unity of action. Local interests would claim their first allegiance. This wide diversity of interest made, at once, the party's difficulty and its opportunity. It is not easy to reproduce the complex situation.

There was Philadelphia, largest city of the State, in the South-East corner, with its large commercial and shipping interests. It enjoyed its monopoly of the trade of all the Eastern portion of the State and had no desire to see communication with the South and West made easy, thus diverting business to Baltimore and Pittsburg. But the great growth of population and its spread throughout the commonwealth inevitably developed an insistent demand for transportation facilities somewhat equally serving each of the sections of the State. It was the period, too, of the development of railroads; and supporters of the canals and waterways made vigorous opposition to any grants of state aid to the new railroads. It was long afterwards that the situation was reversed and the railroads used their power in courts and legislatures and in Congress itself to throttle all development of the waterways.

A glance at a map shows the upper tier of counties physiographically separated from the rest of the state; not benefited by its canals; and at this time, not reached by the railroads; more naturally in communication with New York and more interested in the Erie and Chenango canals than in those of their own state. The lower tier of counties was dependent on traffic East and West, which the canal (running parallel to the North) would compete with and tend to destroy. The Western tier of counties was separated from the rest of the State by the mountain wall of the Alleghenies and sorely needed transportation connections with the East. While a great part of central Pennsylvania was more naturally tributary to Baltimore markets, its interests lay to the south along the Susquehanna. It urged the incorporation and building of the Susquehanna and Baltimore Railroad, stretching from the Maryland line to some elegible point in the Cumberland Valley, as the plan to afford the region its greatest benefit. When a bill was introduced into the Legislature making a grant of $3,000,-000 to this road, its opponents heatedly answered that the Bill ought to be entitled, "An act to vest in Maryland control of all trade with Central Pennsylvania."

With all these conflicting interests before the legislature, the Anti-Mason members voted generally with their local sections; with the result that there could be no very strong party spirit, nor any growing enthusiasm. This was manifest when the state convention was held at Harrisburg in May, 1831; when but half the counties of the State were represented. However, as time for the election drew near, the familiar agitation began again. Anti-Masonic papers were established in the German localities; Morganic books, almanacs without number, with reading matter condemning Masonry, and ridiculous Masonic pictures were peddled and distributed. In the election which followed, there was little change in the strength of the party. Again in 1832, year of the election of President and Governor, local and general issues were all mingled with the Anti-Masonic issue; and as was true wherever the party seemed to make any demonstration of power, its success was due to the refuge it offered to the discontented of all parties and classes, and as affording direct opposition to Jackson. Ritner was again nominated for Governor and his election urged on the grounds that he was Anti-Masonic; that he would save the people from heavy taxes by refusing the large grants which Governor Wolf had recommended for the canals and railroads; that he would give to the western part of the state the relief in transportation so sorely needed.

The state election was held in October, a month preceding the presidential election; but the larger national interests had their weightier part in the campaign. The fact that William Wirt, a German by descent had been nominated for the Presidency by the Anti-Masonic Convention, was stressed in all the German districts in the hope that it would aid the state ticket. Ritner was defeated by a very narrow margin, receiving 88,186 votes; while Governor Wolf received 91,315. This demonstration of party strength led the state committee of the National Republican Party (whose candidate was Henry Clay) to call a hurried convention to meet at Harrisburg on October 16, to endorse the electoral ticket of the Anti-Masonic party. The convention adopted these resolutions:

"Resolved, That to preserve the Constitution of our beloved country and to enable the Anti-Jackson party of Pennsylvania to present a united front in the approaching election, this convention resolves to withdraw the electoral ticket adopted at their session in May last.

"Resolved, That this convention adopt the electoral ticket formed by the Anti-Jackson Convention which assembled at Harrisburg on the anniversary of the birthday of Washington, in February last, and earnestly recommend that ticket to the support of the National Republican Party."

The ticket was sufficiently identified in the resolutions, though the name Anti-Masonic was euphemized to Anti-Jackson. There is every reason to believe that if the ticket had been successful, and Henry Clay had needed these votes to make his election possible, they would have been cast for him. He carried the state with 90,983 votes; while his opponent polled 66,716 votes.

Following this election, there was a decided lull in the activities of the Anti-Masons. Yet the year 1833 had one incident that was to make an entire change in the spirit and vigor of the movement. This was the election of Thaddeus Stevens to the legislature. Stevens was one of those tireless, indefatigable workers who, given a cause that commands their heart and conscience, will move heaven and earth to make it succeed. It was largely due to his zeal and skillful handling and persistent labors that the Anti-Masonic movement revived and pressed on until it controlled the government of the State. Stevens marked his entrance on the floor of the legislature by offering a resolution, which would have made Freemasonry a legal ground for peremptory challenge to jurors in all cases where a Mason was involved. It also provided that in the prosecution of a criminal case, if the defendant and judge were both Masons the same provision should apply that now exists in cases where the judge and one of the parties are related by blood or marriage. The bill was defeated, but it started a fresh and bitter attack on Masonry.

Stevens continued the fight by offering a bill which made criminal the taking of extra-judicial oaths. Another bill was introduced, entitled, "Act to suppress secret societies bound together by secret and unlawful oaths." The first section imposed a fine of $100 on any person administering an oath to another initiate into any society or being advanced from one degree to another. Every person present when such an oath was administered is made a witness and compelled to testify. The second section of the bill required all bodies of Masons and Odd Fellows to make annual report of their officers and members, with the names of those admitted during the year, together with the form of promises or obligations that have been administered during their initiation. Addressing the House, Stevens demanded that Governor Wolf, a Mason, be brought before the House to answer as to how far Masonry had affected his political appointments; and as to how many felons whom he had pardoned, had been "brethren of the mystic tie." He proposed also to hale before the House the judges to ascertain whether the "Grand hailing sign had been ever handed, sent, or thrown to them by either of the parties litigant; and if so, what had been the result of the trial." The House met his measures by tabling his motions. He then gave notice that he would call up the matter every day until action was taken. His persistence finally succeeded, at least in part; for his resolution was permitted to pass with the terms, "Masons" and "Odd Fellows" omitted; and the words "Secret Societies" inserted instead.

He labored constantly to unite all the forces that were opposed to the Democrats, and by this combination was enabled to effect a good deal of legislation. Among the legislation with which he must be credited was the bill in support of the public schools. The Quakers, the German bodies, the Presbyterians all maintained their own schools and so were unwilling to be taxed heavily for public education. Public sentiment, however had long desired a change. Governor Wolf in all his messages brought the matter to the attention of the Legislature. Stevens had been elected largely by German votes opposed to this school legislation, yet he did not hesitate to champion the cause of the schools and it was his powerful assistance that prevented amendment to the bill that would have ruined the school system by pauperizing it. He declared that if his position on the question was considered a serious detriment to his party, "He would withdraw from the county which had honored him by election to the legislature to find some place where the advocates of Anti-Masonry may be advocates of knowledge."

After a very bitter campaign, with three candidates for Governor, Ritner was elected by a large plurality. He received 94,023 votes; Wolf, 65,804; and Mulenberg, 40,586. Thus in six years after its first campaign in the state, the Anti-Masonic party had elected its Governor and in combination with its allies was in control of the legislature. They proceeded at once to use their power.

Stevens at once introduced a bill providing for the suppression of secret societies bound together by unlawful oaths and was himself appointed chairman of a committee to investigate the evils of Freemasonry with authority to summon witnesses. He first called ex-Governor George Wolf, who denied his authority and refused to appear. Stevens then asked that "attachments issue to compel the delinquent witnesses to attend." After bitter debate this was passed and on January 18, 1836, amid intense excitement, the witnesses were brought before the Committee for examination.

The people crowded into the room to hear the secrets of Freemasonry revealed; men fought for a chance to get within hearing distance. His opponents called it "The Old Woman's Curiosity Convention," with Stevens as Chief "Old Woman." Others compared it to the "Inquisition" with Stevens as "Chief Inquisitor."

But great was the disappointment of the crowd for the witnesses when called, either simply refused to answer; or read dignified protests against the procedure. Stevens was beside himself with anger and secured the adoption of an order directing the Sergeant-at-arms to take into custody twenty-five recalcitrant witnesses and to hold them until delivered by due course of law. But his followers were getting weary of this fruitless persecution and after a struggle voted to discharge the prisoners. Stevens submitted with bad grace, threatening to carry his appeal to the people, declaring that he would finally "crush that polluting Order or go down to the grave never faltering in a righteous cause." The year quickly passed with the Anti-Masonic Whig party in the legislature passing a number of popular measures. They chartered The Bank and by the terms of the charter, the State received a bonus of $4,500,000, together with $700,000 for certain improvements. The legislature proceeded to distribute this sum among all the various sectional improvements, canals, railroads, turnpikes, etc., winning many adherents to the party.

As the presidential election again drew near, Stevens and the radical Anti-Masons secured from each of the prominently mentioned candidates a statement as to their position on the Masonic question. They were not satisfied with the statements of any of those who were seeking the Whig nomination and so insisted on the party putting up a distinctly Anti-Masonic candidate. They were able to carry with them only the extremists of the party and as other states were not favorable to the holding of a convention, they were left no other alternative but to support Harrison who had been named by the Whigs. The Democrats named Martin Van Buren and this brought on a renewal of the Anti-Catholic spirit which had been manifested in Pennsylvania in the three-cornered gubernatorial contest of 1835. Van Buren was accused of being too friendly with the Pope and with many Catholics. The *Pennsylvania Intelligencer* of September 15, 1836, printed the following:

"Van Buren and the Pope! For the first time candidate for the first office in the land, he comes before the people as the correspondent of the Pope of Rome, as the fawning sycophantic flatterer of a foreign tyrant—for the purpose of arraying one religious denomination against another—of making a sectarian party in politics and of securing the influence of what he impudently calls the 'Holy Father' upon the Catholics of the United States, to unite in a body in politics. In a letter to the Pope, Martin acknowledges the Pope to be the 'head of the great Christian Church' and offered congratulations to the Holy Father upon his recent accession to the Tiara!"

In this election, the Anti-Masonic Party, with the exception of its extreme devotees, was completely absorbed into the growing Whig Party. Stevens was defeated for the Legislature and so the attacks upon Masonry lost their sharpest sting. Governor Ritner, in his message of 1836, made one more determined attack on the fraternity, seeking to dim the glory of Washington's active connection as a Mason. He argued that what was a comparatively harmless institution in Washington's day, had grown to be a powerful, oath-bound, secret-working society. He declared his belief that the new legislature met under peculiarly favorable circumstances for the final disposal of the unpleasant matter. He called upon them to make full investigation and then to pass laws for the complete suppression of the stumbling block. The Democratic majority in the legislature refused to do his bidding and in turn demanded his authority for his denial of Washington's warm adherence to the fraternity.

The attack served one valuable service. It led to a most important contribution to Masonic literature by Ezra Lincoln in the *Vindication of George Washington*, published in Boston, 1841.

Thus ends a unique period in the political history of Pennsylvania. The Anti-Masonic spirit did not immediately die out; it continued spasmodically to show itself for many years, especially in the western part of the state where it connected itself with the temperance, the anti-slavery, and anti-Catholic movements. To Thaddeus Stevens must be given the credit of reviving the movement when it was fading away in 1832-1833. As McCarty says in his study of the period, "The great fact in the history of Anti-Masonry in Pennsylvania is the personality of Thaddeus Stevens —the Yankee leader of Pennsylvania Quakers, Scotch Presbyterians, and German Sectarians."

CHAPTER VIII

ANTI-MASONRY IN NEW ENGLAND

EARLY New England had a conscience all its own; it may have been narrow, but there was the strength of its rocks and hills in its rugged devotion to conviction. Its social life in town and country centered in the church. Its weekly newspapers contained less of political than of religious discussion. The "Town Meeting" was the forum where public opinion crystallized; where news was distributed; where the voice of the people had free expression and where local government was administered. This peculiar feature of the social life of New England made it a fruitful field for the propagandists of Anti-Masonry. When the Morgan story had been vividly told, and the guilt of his abductors or murderers apparently fixed on members of the fraternity, the reaction was swift and far-reaching.

In Maine, there was a general secession of members from their lodges; charters were forfeited and there came a year (1830) when the Grand Junior Warden was the only officer present at the annual meeting of the Grand Lodge; not a single lodge was regularly represented; and the only attendants were eight faithful and unafraid brethren of Portland who came as visitors to show their loyalty.

Masonry in the new world, had been first established in Massachusetts. In colonial days, the spirit of liberty and devotion to the Revolutionary cause had been nurtured in Masonic lodges and around the Masonic Altars. Many of the thrilling incidents of the outbreak of the Revolution had Masonic associations— The Boston Tea Party, Paul Revere's ride, Bunker Hill with its noble and heroic Warren. The strong men of the state had been members and leaders of the fraternity. It is difficult to believe that a state which had known the true spirit of Masonry as manifested in the lives of so many of its distinguished sons, which had contributed so much to the life of Masonry in America, could ever have been carried away by the Anti-Masonic movement. And, indeed, the movement never was as strong in Massachusetts as in the other New England states or in New York and Pennsylvania.

Samuel Greene, Morgan's neighbor, friend and eulogizer, brought the story direct to Boston. In Faneuil Hall he gave a lecture, afterward repeated throughout the State and the whole of New England, which greatly inflamed the public mind. In June, 1828, there was published the first number of the *Boston Free Press,* and a little later the Anti-Masonic *Christian Herald,* both bitterly antagonistic to the fraternity. In its prospectus the *Herald* announced that "it would give a general view of the progress of evangelical religion throughout the world, while its columns would be open to cool and candid discussion of Freemasonry." Within another year, Boston had four papers devoted largely to the incitement of sentiment against the Masonic fraternity.

Masons followed their usual custom of refusing to indulge in open discussion of matters affecting the craft; but at last it was deemed wise to issue a formal defense. In 1831 a statement was prepared and signed by 1469 Masons. These signers were from fifty-four townships; Boston furnished the larger number, 437, but all parts of the State were worthily represented. They denied unequivocally any knowledge or connection with the Morgan affair, either as to his removal or as to the defense of those accused in the case. They asserted the irreproachable character of Masonic principles. They challenged a denial of the fact, that the membership of the fraternity included the best elements of the citizenship of the State. They solemnly averred that no obligation, assumed by Masons in any degree, bound him to sustain a brother in acts which were at variance with the fundamental principles of morality or incompatible with one's duty as a good and faithful citizen.

The legislature took cognizance of the statement and appointed a committee to investigate the Order and to make a reply. This committee presented its report to the Anti-Masonic Convention held in Worcester in September, 1832. The report, in its 38 sections, reiterated all the familiar charges and condemned the Grand Lodge of Massachusetts because it had not disfellowshipped the Masonic bodies of New York for their failure to purge themselves of the Morgan conspirators. Strangely enough, there was intermingled with their terms of "criminal" and "murderers" as applied to these Masons accused in the Morgan case, a section that paid high tribute to their character—Section 16, "That forty-three of the most active criminals involved in the case were men of high respectability and standing, comprising officers of justice, and belonging to almost every occupation and trade and to three of the learned professions; and that the murderers themselves were men of no mean consideration."

To the unbiased reader, there comes at once the reflection of the improbability that so diabolical a conspiracy could have been devised and carried through by men of such high character and standing.

The three great leaders of thought in Massachusetts during this period were Daniel Webster, William Everett and John Quincy Adams. Webster, *facile princeps* of the orators and statesmen of his day, was wrapt up in great national problems; fighting in the United States Senate, with all his magnificent powers of intellect and eloquence, the battle for the preservation of the Union. The Anti-Masonic movement, to him, was but a passing incident. He had personally withheld any application for membership in the Order from a doubt as to the righteousness of its oaths and obligations; and because of his conviction that the supremacy of the laws of the land was the highest, surest bond of union for citizens of the Republic. He was little interested in political Anti-Masonry.

William Everett, cultured, scholarly, quiet and restrained in manner, was not a man to be swept off his feet by this tumult and alarm about the peril to the nation from Freemasonry.

John Quincy Adams had taken a more active interest in the question because his interests in his second campaign for the Presidency, were so vitally affected by the movement in the great states of New York and Pennsylvania. Studious and deliberate in all his habits of thought and life, he delved deeply into the history of the Morgan case and subsequent trials; and became convinced that Morgan was murdered; that too many Masons of different communities were involved to permit the conclusion that it was the hasty act of a few overzealous men; that there must be in the Institution itself, in its obligations, in its secrecy, its exclusiveness, elements that tended inevitably to abuse of privilege, to oppression of others, and to the violation of the rights of uninitiates which our Constitution guarantees without favor to all men. His position in the matter, which was stated with great clearness and fullness in his voluminous correspondence with Col. William L. Stone (Editor of the *New York Commercial and Advertiser*) doubtless had a large influence in developing the sentiment in his State which opposed the fraternity.

But all these men were more interested in national issues and in the National Republican Party than they were in Anti-Masonry, and only dealt with it as the spirit of the day necessitated.

Masonry was not put to rout in Massachusetts as it was in Vermont and Maine. Its lodges still maintained their activities and presented to their foes a militant attitude. It was their numbers and their influence in the Republican State Convention (1833) that defeated Adams for the nomination for Governor, greatly to his humiliation. The same influence caused the defeat of every Anti-Masonic candidate for Governor whom the party placed in the field. Finally in 1836, when the National Republican party fused with the Whigs, the Anti-Masonic party simply disappeared, absorbed in the larger, more comprehensive, more truly national party.

New Hampshire was affected by the same wave of hostility to Masonry that swept over other states; but for some reason, Masonry stood firmer there than in neighboring states. True, there were many withdrawals. When the Grand Lodge met in 1832 for its regular Annual Convocation, the Grand Master did not appear. The minutes, however, make no record of his defection. They simply record the fact that the Deputy Grand Master presided and that in due time, election was held as usual and entire corps of officers for the new year were installed. The minutes show that there were lodges in distress from numerous withdrawals, and unable to meet their financial obligations. The Grand Lodge quietly dealt in turn with each emergency; but paused long enough to make an appropriation of $200, as a patriotic contribution toward the erection of Bunker Hill Monument.

Vermont had the unenviable distinction of yielding most completely to the Anti-Masonic uproar. There were national leaders and statesmen here, with ambitions dependent on the larger national issues to restrain partisan friends and hold them loyal to the National Republican Party which had such controlling influence in Vermont. The people of the State were therefore left free to follow, in the political arena, their passions as aroused by the Anti-Masonic campaign. Ministers, for a time, preached little else than the essentially Satanic nature of the Masonic lodge. Churches, Boards of Deacons, combed their membership, to require of Masons renunciation of the Order. Lodge after lodge surrendered its charter, until every lodge in the state was either charterless or dormant; and the Grand Lodge ceased for a time to hold its meetings.

As early as 1827, the *Danville North Star* was devoting its columns to the attacks on Masonry. On August 25, 1829, the first State Convention was held. Agitators from New York, Rev. Nathaniel Colver, an Anti-Masonic lecturer, and Henry Dana Ward, Editor of the *Anti-Masonic Review*, were present and by their addresses stirred the convention to a high pitch of enthusiasm. Candidates for Governor and for the legislature were named and the campaign entered upon with fiery determination. Many wild charges and rumors kept the voters in a constant state of excitement. At Woodstock, a man named Cutter made an affidavit before the Magistrate that while in New York in July, he had met one Joseph Burnham who had been convicted of some crime, and imprisoned and was supposed to have died before his term expired. Cutter claimed to have known Burnham intimately and declared there could be no mistake in his identification of the man in New York. Burnham was a Mason and the Superintendent of the prison was a Mason. The inference was plain. Burnham had been given his liberty through Masonic appeal; and the story of his death had been concocted to conceal the fraud. The legislature then in session, appointed a committee of investigation. A visit to New York and interview with the man whom Cutter had identified as Burnham, developed that it was a case of mistaken identity. The Anti-Masons were not satisfied. The grave in which Burnham was supposed to have been buried was opened, the body disinterred; an inquest held and the widow identified it as the body of her husband. All this caused feverish excitement until the story was exploded; after that the Masons used it to heap ridicule on their foes. On election day, they polled 7400 votes and elected thirty-three out of a total of 214 members of the legislature; their candidate for Governor, meanwhile, having declined the honor.

In the election of the following year (1830) there was a sufficient increase of the Anti-Masonic vote to prevent a majority for either of the three candidates for Governor. Crafts, National Republican, received 13,486 votes; William A. Palmer, Anti-Masonic, 10,-925; and Meech, Democratic, 6,285.

During the following five years, the party showed ever increasing strength in the State. In June, 1831.

the State Convention met at Montpelier and again nominated Palmer for Governor. Among the resolutions adopted by the convention was one declaring, "We consider adherence to Masonry is a disqualification for any responsible office in the state or nation." Another declared, "The Convention views with regret and astonishment the influence of Masonry throughout the Union—that no man is duly qualified for the Presidency unless he is a high Mason, a murderer and a duelist." Again there was no majority for either of the candidates; but Palmer had a plurality of twenty-five hundred votes and was elected by the legislature.

The year 1832 was the Presidential election year and the campaign was bitterly personal. Clay (National Republican) and Jackson (Democrat) were both Masons. The one was attacked for alleged corruption of his personal life; the other for his high-handed, autocratic defiance of law and constitution in the pursuit of his purposes. William Wirt, Anti-Masonic candidate for the Presidency, had been a Jefferson supporter, Attorney General in the Cabinet of John Quincy Adams, and was now living in retirement in Baltimore. Wirt swept the State (the only State in the Union to give him its electoral vote), receiving 13,106 votes; Clay, 11,152; and Jackson, 7,780.

In 1833 and 1834, the Anti-Masons with Governor Palmer as their candidate still maintained their control of the State government; but in 1835 his vote began to dwindle. He still had a plurality but it was impossible to combine with the Whig members of the legislature in support of his election. After many fruitless ballots, Jennison, Anti-Masonic Lieutenant Governor, was chosen Governor.

As in New York, Pennsylvania and Massachusetts, the year 1836 saw the movement in New England as a spent force. Its passing was somewhat softened by alliance with the growing Whig Party; but this alliance was in reality an absorption of the once powerful, now decadent, Anti-Masonic body. In a few years it was only a memory and the voters returned to their allegiance to one or the other of the great parties builded on broader national issues and principles. Everywhere, except in the first blaze of resentment against Masonry for its real or fancied wrongdoing, the Anti-Masonic Party on its own issue failed to command any wide support.

If there is any lesson clearly taught by the experience of the rise and growth and decline of Anti-Masonry it is this:—that no party builded on prejudice can long endure. No party, whose controlling impulse is an attack on another body of citizens because of their personal beliefs or social relationships, can hope to develop controlling national strength.

Our American Government rests on broader foundations of liberty and justice and right. Our American citizenship is too jealous of its personal rights and liberties to permit such oppression. Within the Constitution, our liberties must be secure. President William Henry Harrison was right when, as a candidate, he was urged by Thaddeus Stevens to say that if elected he would use all his power to suppress Masonry, and made answer: "I am certain there exists no power, either in the government as a whole or in any of its departments to effect that suppression; I am sure that the attempt to exercise it would constitute an usurpation of power, pregnant, if tolerated by the people, with mischief infinitely more fatal, than that which it was intended to remedy."

Excitement and prejudice may sway one group; resentment against real or fancied wrong may inflame another; but we are a nation, a people. Many strains of blood have flowed into our common Americanism; but they have united to make one people. The common hope and common sense of the great American people will ever refuse to submit to bigotry and prejudice. They may be counted on to make effective resistance to any group or any party or any spirit that thinks to sway the nation by such means.

CHAPTER IX

THE SECRECY OF MASONRY

THE element of mystery has always had its fascination for mankind.

What lies beyond the mountains? Some youth is certain to climb the topmost peak to discover that beyond his familiar narrow valley, there stretches a great bright world of enchantment.

What lies beyond the sea? Some intrepid mariner will face wind and wave and unknown elements until he has sailed his circling bark around the globe, and faced the peoples of unknown tongues.

Whither leads yon star? And though all else say the journey is too far, the desert to be crossed too hot and barren, the home ties too alluring, there is always some Caspar, Melchior, Balthazzar or Artaban who, to make the grand discovery, will hazard life and limb and treasure to follow the star till it comes to rest over the chamber of infinite love.

What is the secret of life? It is even a vapor that passeth away; a shuttle flying to and fro; a tale that is told; a watch in the night; intangible, mysterious, inexplicable.

> "Between two worlds life hovers like a star,
> 'Twixt night and morn, upon the horizon's verge.
> How little do we know that which we are!"

Yet still some Mahatma or Plato or St. Paul will seek to solve that mystery, bringing to bear upon the problem all the powers of known philosophy and all religion, while a Flexner or a Kelvin with biological microscope or scalpel will seek to pierce to the origin of all.

What lies beyond the grave? And even the arch-doubter confesses, "We stand between the barren peak of two eternities; we seek to pierce beyond the veil; but have no answer from the darkness, save the echo of our cry."

Mystery! The very word itself is an interesting study. For us it signifies that which is unknown and unexplained; that which baffles our intellects or our senses. But that was not the original meaning of the word. It was brought over bodily from the Greek—*musterion*. In ancient Greece they had their guilds and schools and brotherhoods, each with its own peculiar philosophy of life and duty and happiness; its doctrine of man's relation to his fellow and his God. These creeds and philosophies of life were for the initiates only, who shared and sympathized with them. To converse privately, uninterrupted by the throng upon the streets or by those not in harmony, upon these themes, gave infinite satisfaction, as two lovers, with hearts atune, find infinite pleasure in choosing one star for their star; one tree of the forest; unknown to all the world beside, as their trysting place.

Then, too, this secrecy of creed and philosophy of life served to prevent admittance of the ignorant or unsympathetic or unworthy mortals who would only have vexed and disturbed the calm spirit of the brotherhood. Yet some inkling of this secret bond of faith and hope and fellowship must be allowed to reach men in the outer world; else, how could new recruits and worthy additions to the brotherhood be found? So brief, epigrammatic mottoes, indicative of the vital purpose—the secret truth—flung out as a banner to the world. This motto, revealing that which was concealed, the essence of the secret life was the "musterion," the Mystery. So did St. Paul thrust out his magnet into that hostile heathen world, to attract kindred souls to his Gospel. "Great," he says, "is the musterion of Godliness—God manifest in the flesh, justified in the spirit, seen of angels, preached unto the gentiles, believed on in the world, received up into glory."

Freemasonry, following the sure instinct of the great teachers of the race, throws the veil of mystery about its Temple; half conceals, half discloses those ideals, that mystic light and truth that are the glory of our humanity. By the very mystery it would lure men to the quest. Were the privileges of Masonry to be bestowed indiscriminately, the very objects of its being would be subverted; being too familiar, would lose their attractiveness and sink into disregard. It is one of the traits of our human nature that we value that for which we must seek; and difficulty of attainment but adds to our sense of value. Lessing says, "The value to man does not consist in the truth which he possesses, but in the sincere pains that he hath taken to find it out. His powers do not augment by possessing truth, but by investigating it. For possession lulls the energies of man, and makes him idle and proud." Masonry but uses the natural instinct of men; robes the truth in beautiful symbol; lets the light enter gradually, as veil after veil unfolds to reveal all that God hath shown us of human need and human brotherhood; only asking that the form and method of this revealing shall be reserved for those who indicate a purpose to walk in harmony and keep the faith.

Let it be made clear, that this secrecy does not extend to our principles or purposes or ideals. One of the most frequent charges against the fraternity, is based on this element of secrecy. "Secret, oath-bound Order" was a phrase that suggested to the hostile critic, purposes dark and dangerous and criminal. From one point of view, Masonry is not a secret order. The *Vehm Gerichte* in the countries along the bank of the Rhine was a secret order. No one knew who were its members; if one thought he knew, he must speak of it in a whisper. They met in secret. They were masked, so that one could not know who sat by his side. They met as a court with life and death in their hands; yet none knew who was accused nor who was accuser. The *Devorants* was a secret society of Paris. Its members were unknown. The public could not discover that they ever met. They never announced the purpose of their existence. Only they knew anything about it, who, by chance, came into cross purposes with one of its members. Then it was discovered by a series of mysterious, powerful, relentless acts, all tending to the one purpose and that the will of the offended one, that the contest was not with one alone, but with his numerous and unknown allies. In every land, in every age, there have been these secret societies. But Masonry is not secret in any such sense. Its members are known. Its halls are massive buildings. Its meetings are regularly held and freely advertised. Men glory in their membership. They appear in public in their regalia. Their ancient charges and constitution are published and may be read by all. They have their public functions. A great body of literature is to be found on the shelves of every public library, historical, explanatory, expository. They proclaim as from the house tops their three great principles— Brotherly Love, Relief and Truth. With solemn step, unembarrassed by display of distinctive aprons and gloves, they keep company with a brother to his grave. Masonry has no mysteries of iniquity. With ignoble deeds of darkness, it has no sympathy. What the world has the right to know, is freely made known. But there are sanctities in every home; there are privacies in every life, into which the world has no right to peep with prying eyes. So Masonry reserves to itself its time honored privacies, knowledge of which is the open sesame into the brotherhood the world around.

It was the fear that these lawful privacies were to be invaded, these sacred rites and tokens of the Brotherhood to be spread broadcast to the world, that so aroused the Masons of 100 years ago against William Morgan. They feared that the betrayal of Masonic secrets would mean the eventual extinction of the Order. There are knaves in every human organization; there was a Judas Iscariot in the company of the Master's disciples. There have been many wretched men, through all the years, who for hope of monetary gain or in revenge for fancied slight or wrong, have thought to bring down the pillars of our temple by printing what they could remember of Masonic forms and ceremonies. Masons have been content to trust to the common sense and good faith of upright sensible men to give a fair judgment of the value of these pretended revelations of the wanton perjurers. Masonry rests not on these secret forms. It is a life. It is a spirit. It is a character. No one can deprive another of it. No one can unmake a true Mason; for what makes him a Mason is not some word he has heard, some scene which he has witnessed; but some truth of God which he has made his own, some moral strength which has become the very fibre of his life and soul. When a man has been initiated, passed and raised and has signed the by-laws, in a sense he is a Master Mason. He is numbered in the membership, and is entitled to wear the badge. But in reality, he has only been given the right to enter the Temple. Whether he does enter or no, whether he labors on that spiritual building or stands idly within the shadow and shelter of its walls, time alone will tell. But it depends wholly upon himself. He has found the true secret of Masonry, if he has learned that God is his Father and men about him are his brethren; and if that knowledge mellows and purifies his soul, inspires his deeds and radiates a sunny glory from his life.

CHAPTER X

MASONRY SURVIVES THE STORM

AFTER the tempest has spent its fury and the wind has subsided and peaceful calm has settled down upon the great deep, the mariner makes careful examination to discover the damage which has been done. He notes whether the mast has been loosened from its fastenings; what sails have been carried away; what cords need to be replaced; what seams in the hull have been opened up.

The attack on Masonry had its threefold basis:

1. Honest, sincere revulsion of sentiment against fraternity because of the Morgan incident. Many true Masons said, "Show me that Morgan was murdered and that any Masonic Body was responsible for the crime, and I will renounce the institution forever."

2. There was active and unscrupulous use of the incident for political purposes. It has been shown that the old Federal Party had disintegrated; plainly a new party of opposition must inevitably develop. Ambitious men were eager to grasp the reins of governmental place and power. This Masonic agitation came at the opportune moment. Masonry was widespread, reaching out to every city, town and hamlet in the land. Its membership included most of the leaders of the party in power. The situation seemed to offer an easy road to success. To inflame the people against the

fraternity was to forge a force that would sweep the country.

3. The widespread discussion about Masonry had aroused a questioning in the minds of men who had given little thought to the subject, as to its merits or demerits. Many men had gone into it rather unthinkingly, carried in by its tide of popular favor. In a day of rather narrow and intolerant religious spirit, the accusation that Masonry was incompatible with vital Christian faith turned some worthy men against it.

These three elements of antagonism must all be considered in seeking any true measure of the lasting effect of this ten years of intense and bitter propaganda. With respect to the first, it should be said that Masons throughout the country were conscious of absolute innocence of any activity or participation in the Morgan affair. They knew that the principles of the Order demanded moral conduct above reproach. No body of men would be more insistent in exacting of all men, and particularly of Masons, the highest ethical standards. Moreover the members of the fraternity were known in their communities as men of high standing; and the public could not long be deceived into believing that such men could be guilty of murder and treason. Therefore, after there was time for sober reflection, that first element of attack was certain to fail; it could not permanently injure the Order. "Thrice armed is he, who has his quarrel just."

It has been clearly shown that the attempt to make political capital out of the Morgan incident, was doomed to speedy collapse. The voters might be swept off their feet by vitriolic condemnation and untempered accusation. But the sober sense of our citizenship was sure after a while to assert itself in stubborn unbelief of charges against an organization that was both ancient and honorable; whose whole history, in the old world and the new, was a denial of the possibility of such a reversion of character, such a turning topsy-turvy of conduct and established reputation. Moreover, a personal incident, or a matter affecting a society, forms too small and narrow a basis on which to project a great national party in a day when the vital questions of the liberties and rights of men were at stake; and when the Senate was debating the question of the very existence of the Union.

That third element of attack was the one charge of an enduring nature, and that went to the root of the matter. Was Masonry essentially a force for righteousness, or a power of evil in the community? Did it lower the character of men, or did it tend to strengthen all the forces of righteousness in the individual and the state? That question had to be squarely met, and honestly and satisfactorily answered, if Masonry was to survive and be restored to its former place of prestige and honor.

One powerful factor in the gradual and sure progress of the public mind to a sane, sound attitude on the Masonic matter, was the unflinching fidelity of some of its strong leaders. President Andrew Jackson was not swerved an iota from his loyalty to Masonry.

"The Masonic Society," he wrote in the very thick of the fight, "is an institution calculated to benefit mankind and I trust it will continue to prosper." Henry Clay, Jackson's opponent for the Presidency, might have benefited greatly; but he positively refused to be identified with the Anti-Masonic Party. Stephen Van Rensselaer, respected member of the old Dutch aristocracy, was chosen Grand Master when the Order was at low ebb in New York. "If I consulted my own inclination and feelings, I should unhesitatingly decline the honor," he wrote, in response to a note informing him of his election. "But when I consider the unmerited abuse of the Order by designing men, and the persecutions of our brethren, I will consent to accept, if my acceptance is deemed of any importance to the cause."

Then there was given to the public a series of sober, strong, statements in defence, that were in such contrast to the malignant attacks, that thoughtful men were favorably impressed. On June 24, 1830, Grand Master Morgan Lewis issued an address on assuming his office. In a paper that was replete with fine sentiments, he said: "Believing that no favorable result can be expected from reasoning with men during paroxisms of feverish imaginations, stimulated in many instances by hope of personal gain, I exhort the Brethren to follow the example of the fathers; regardless of slanders and revilings by our enemies to pursue the even tenor of their way; deviating neither to the right hand nor to the left; but like Stern's monk, looking straight forward, to something beyond this world."

In 1830, a memorial was presented to the legislature of Rhode Island, urging legislation that would completely suppress the Order within the state. In reply, the Grand Lodge wrote, "We fully accord to our opponents the right of free men to memorialize the government in opposition to our interests as Masons. But we should be wanting in self-respect if we did not exercise the inalienable right of self-defence. We challenge the strictest scrutiny and offer the greatest facility of investigation. It is urged that we have secrets, not to be disclosed but at 'the hazard of life.' We admit we have secrets, but none that can be disclosed only at 'the hazard of life.' No doubt the memorialists had their eye on the supposed murder of William Morgan by Masons. Of that supposed act, we can neither affirm nor deny; for we know nothing about it. We appeal to the Great Searcher of hearts to test our sincerity, as we assert that we have never received, given, nor countenanced any obligation requiring the sacrifice of life as the penalty for the disclosure of Masonic secrets. We as cordially detest the crime of lawless murder as any other body of men. We hold no fellowship with any man or body of men, to our knowledge and belief, who would either perpetrate it themselves or sanction it in others. We are citizens of Rhode Island and claim the right enjoyed by all others to be considered innocent until proven guilty; refusing to abide by idle rumor and unsupported attack merely because we happen to be objects of party jealousies. Satisfy us by any tangible evidence that Masonry will be injurious to posterity, we will renounce it; for we yield the palm to no men as to our good wishes for the welfare of future generations." Such a statement, backed up by men of known probity and established integrity, must eventually overpower the mountebanks who went from town to town, lecturing on Anti-Masonry and pretending to give the degrees of Entered Apprentice, Fellow Craft and Master Mason as an evening's entertainment.

But the tide turned slowly. In New York it seemed as if it never would turn. The membership dwindled from 20,000 in 1826 to about 3000 in 1836. In 1832, the Grand Secretary, in announcing the vote on a new Constitution, said there were only 48 lodges entitled to votes. That year 84 lodges lost their charters. The next year 110 charters were rescinded. In 1836, a different tone sounds through the minutes. There is an item, Morton Lodge No. 63 (which had been suspended) now reports 15 members loyal and true and they request the restoration of their Masonic privileges. Rising Sun Lodge No. 185 made a similar request and its charter was restored. In 1838, in beginning his address, the Grand Secretary said, "I have great pleasure in communicating to the Grand Lodge, that the general condition and prospects of the Masonic Order are highly satisfactory. The tide of prosperity is rising and flowing up the rivers to the North and West. Our remotest frontier lodges are again at work." There were then perhaps 50 lodges in the State in good standing. In 1839, the Grand Lodge ordered a renumbering of the lodges and this corrected list showed a real gain during the year; though the high number now was No. 72, while before the Anti-Masonic campaign the high number had been 507.

In 1842, the tone of the Grand Master's Annual Address was actually cheerful. He began, "I am happy to be able to congratulate you on the prosperous condition of the Institution throughout the world and, especially, on the favorable progress of events throughout our own country." In 1847, Masonic addresses had begun to speak of the Masonic agitation and decline as a past period; interesting as an historical study, but as distinctly ended, and a new era of confidence and progress began. In his address that year, Grand Master Willard said, "A kind and beneficent Providence has watched over our destiny through the year. It is only a few years since we witnessed the excitement and delusion in relation to our Order which swept the land like a pestilence. In this trying ordeal, faint-hearted and unworthy members of the Craft were winnowed out and borne away like chaff before the winds. But the body of the Fraternity has stood fast in their integrity. My Brethren, we are now reaping the reward of our constancy. Freemasonry is again held in respect and honor; our halls are crowded with candidates and the Society holds its just rank among the social and benevolent institutions of the State. Let us profit by the lesson which experience has taught us, and guard with constant vigilance the portals of the Masonic Temple; permitting none to enter save those whose pure lives and characters will make them an ornament and support of our ancient Order."

Passing from a review of conditions in New York to that of the New England States, we find the low water mark for the fraternity was reached in Vermont. By 1831, most of the lodges of the State were charterless or too asleep or dead to give up their charters in orderly manner. A paper had been circulated, asking that an emergency meeting of the Grand Lodge be held to consider the orderly dissolution of the Institution of Masonry in the State. When this emergent Grand Lodge met in October, 1831, the solemn and momentous portent of the occasion breathes in the opening words of Grand Master Haswell. "The Almighty and Righteous Governor of the Universe has again permitted us to assemble within these walls which have been dedicated to Him, to Virtue and to Universal Benevolence. We are met to discharge the responsible trust committed to us. We have implored His blessing upon our labors and should in cheerful confidence rely on His support. The question of the dissolution of the Institution of Masonry in this State is now before you. Masonic Lodges have existed in this State for almost a half century. They are older than the State itself. What have Masons done, that this widespread ruin should visit us? We have made repeated and solemn appeals to our fellow citizens, neighbors, and to those endeared to us by ties of kinship and affection. In return we have met with reproach and persecution. Our honest intentions have been misrepresented, our rights as Freemen and Masons abridged, our characters traduced. What shall now be done? Will you permit me to answer? Breast the Storm; and when the calm succeeds, an injured and insulted public will restore us to our rights and visit the despoilers with infamy and disgrace. The eyes of Christians and Philanthropists are upon us watching to see whether we shall surrender our Masonic citadel. This day will decide whether Masonry in Vermont is to stand or fall. Our mountains and everlasting hills, planted by God as monuments of His unchangeableness, should be the emblems of our firmness and moral courage and continued fidelity to our principles and our Altar." The touching appeal was not in vain, for when the vote was taken it resulted in rejecting the proposal of dissolution by an overwhelming vote, ninety-nine to nineteen. On the same day however, the Grand Lodge took action, that, in view of the hostile sentiment existing in the State, lodges should meet but twice a year until a brighter day should dawn; once, for the good of the Order, for discipline, and for Masonic instruction; lest the traditions of Masonry should die out; once, for the election of officers, that the organization might be maintained.

Again in 1833, the same proposal for the dissolution of Masonry in Vermont was voted down in the Grand Lodge. But it was resolved to receive the charters of any lodges that wished voluntarily to surrender them. One interesting provision was made, that any funds in the Treasuries of lodges surrendering their charters should be given to the Public School Fund of the State. In 1836 the Grand Lodge voted to hold, thereafter, only biennial meetings. As a matter of fact, it did not meet again for ten long years. Even the heroic courage and fidelity of Grand Master Haswell and his loyal co-workers were compelled to bend before the fury of the storm of Anti-Masonic sentiment. But in January, 1846, a Convention of Masons met at Burlington and appointed a Committee consisting of Philip Tucker, Samuel S. Tucker, Joel Winch, John Brainerd, James Platt and Anthony Haswell to consider the state of the Order. They reported that the last election of officers in the Grand Lodge had been in 1836; that at the times appointed for the biennial meetings, some of the officers had always met and, finding no quorum, had taken regular adjournment until the next appointed day. So that, their judgment was that the Grand Lodge was still in legal existence, its officers holding over until their successors had been elected and installed. Acting on this authorization, the Grand Officers opened Grand Lodge and proceeded to the discharge of their duties. There were ten lodges represented in the Grand Lodge by their Masters and Wardens: and the minutes note the attendance of a "large and respectable gathering of interested, visiting brethren." Grand Master Haswell, now in more cheerful mood, said in his Address, "With high hopes, with Christian faith and charity, we look to the future. Masonry in other States was never in more flourishing condition than at present. Everywhere, now, the Institution is upheld, honored and respected." He thanked the Grand Officers and Masons of New Hampshire, Massachusetts, Rhode Island, New York, Delaware and Maryland for able counsel and Masonic support "that strengthened our weak and feeble arm in the hour of peril and difficulty." The Grand Lodge repealed the action ordering biennial sessions, and ordered that regular annual meetings be held. The next year, in the report of the Committee on Correspondence of the Grand Lodge, we find these acknowledgments: "Rhode Island cheered us on to our labors. Connecticut extends the right hand of fellowship, Tennessee hails with kindness, Maine, Iowa and Florida acknowledge announcement of our resumption of labor, Kentucky, Illinois and New York raise some question as to the regularity of a Grand Lodge resuming after a ten year interim." But in 1849, the Correspondence Committee reported, twenty-four State Jurisdictions (there were just 24 States at that time), together with the Grand Lodge of the District of Columbia and two Grand Bodies of Canada, had joined in recognition; and so Masonry in Vermont may be said to have finally proved its survival and its right to a place in the sun in the Masonry of the world.

The Masons of New Hampshire had been subjected to the same storm of attack as in other States, but refused to be stampeded into giving up their rights and organization. Yet in 1838, a Committee on the state of the Order reported to the Grand Lodge that only five lodges in the State had done any work in the years from 1828 to 1838. The lodges had met, more or less regularly; usually with a small attendance; maintained their organizations; encouraged their members to be loyal and patient: waiting for the better day.

The solidity and high character of the Masonic Institution in Massachusetts enabled it to make a very strong defense against its foes. It refused to yield any ground; it returned stroke for stroke, blow for blow, with its foes. In conscious integrity, it stood on its rights; from time to time made dignified and thoughtful answer to attacks; and finally wore down the fury of its antagonists, and emerged triumphant for its long career of honor and usefulness in the Commonwealth.

At one stage of the conflict the Grand Lodge decided to surrender to the State its civil Charter. On December 27, 1833, the Committee of the Grand Lodge informed the legislature that the Grand Lodge by formal vote had relinquished its corporate powers and vacated its act of incorporation. But they added, "That there may be no misunderstanding of our position either in the mind of the Legislature or of citizens generally, we beg leave to represent precisely the nature of this surrender. In divesting itself of corporate powers, the Grand Lodge has not relinquished any of its Masonic attributes or prerogatives. These it claims to hold and to exercise independently alike of popular will or legal enactment—not of toleration but of right. Its members are intelligent freemen; and though willing to restore any gift or advantage derived from the Government—when it became the object of jealousies, however unfounded—*nothing is further from our intentions than to sacrifice the interests of the Institution intrusted to our care, in order to appease the popular excitement of which that Institution may have been the innocent 'occasion.'*" Against such firm resistance, the attack wore itself out in Massachusetts long before it did in neighboring States. In 1835, a Board, authorized by the Grand Lodge, repurchased and recovered title to the Masonic Temple in Boston which it had been obliged to give up when it surrendered its civil charter. In making report to the Grand Lodge, this committee said, "We cannot refrain from congratulating our brethren that at the end of this period of controversy, we find our treasury solvent; our resources adequate to the needs of the Institution; but, what is still more tributary to our self-respect, a more precious treasure has been preserved—our honor untarnished and the good faith of our Masonic engagements." Of course not all prejudice had been dissipated, nor all antagonism stilled. Even as late as 1843, it manifested itself in an irritating incident. On June 17 of that year Boston was the scene of a celebration of the completion of Bunker Hill Monument. The President of the United States and his Cabinet and a company of distinguished guests were present. Those in charge of the Jubilee did not feel the propriety of inviting the Grand Lodge of Masons to the ceremonies. The relation of the fraternity to that sacred ground was peculiar and intimate. The first martyr, whose blood had consecrated it, was a distinguished Provincial

Grand Master of Masons of the State, General Joseph Warren. The original monument on the ground had been erected largely as the result of the patriotic activity and generosity of Masons under the leadership of the Grand Lodge; and they had made generous contributions toward the erection of the new monument. All this historic relationship was ignored. The Officers of the Grand Lodge attended as individuals and the affair passed off as acceptably to the fraternity as could be expected under the embarrassing circumstances. But steadily the Order pursued the even tenor of its way, and eventually regained its position of honor and influence.

The minutes of the Grand Lodge of Pennsylvania reveal a remarkable absence of discussion of the Anti-Masonic movement. In this State under the lead of Thaddeus Stevens, political Anti-Masonry reached its climax of bitterness. The reports to Grand Lodge indicate the same conditions as in other affected States. Members were renouncing the Order; lodges giving up their charters, etc. But so substantial a portion of the Fraternity stood steadfast that the Grand Lodge moved quietly on, along its regular lines of business, until the brief spasm of violence had subsided.

It was in Baltimore, Maryland, that the National Convention of the Anti-Masonic Party met in 1832 and nominated a resident of the city, William Wirt, as its candidate for the Presidency. At that time, the city rang with denunciation of Masonry and vilification of Masons. The movement made some headway throughout the State, reducing the activities of lodges to a minimum; in some cases lodges were so reduced in strength and spirit that for a number of years they were entirely dormant. In the neighboring District of Columbia, the same conditions prevailed. Washington Commandery of Knights Templar had been chartered in 1825 and was in its first prime vigor when the wave of hostility swept over it. It struggled to maintain itself, but its minutes are entirely silent for nearly nine years. In November, 1832, the Grand Encampment of Knights Templar and the General Grand Chapter of Royal Arch Masons met in Baltimore. It was like bearding the lion in his den, to come to this city where the opposition to Masonry had flung out its national political banner. But now in November, the frenzy was past; the Anti-Masonic Party had made its pitiful national showing; Jackson, the Mason, had been elected to the Presidency. The night of agony was passing. The darkness lingered for a period, but the light began to break. The Grand Encampment made its defiant proclamation: "Political bodies, in assailing the Orders of Knighthood, have aimed a blow at the free institutions of the country and at the inalienable rights of a free people." It is interesting to recall that nearly forty years later, the same city thronged its streets, brilliantly decorated with flags and insignia of the Order, to welcome the Triennial Conclave of the Templars with the heartiest greetings and most liberal sentiments of approval.

Mention of conditions in one more State, seriously

affected by the Anti-Masonic movement, must close this chapter on Masonry's Survival. Masonry had been planted in Michigan in the middle colonial period. In 1760, the British troops had captured Canada and taken possession of Detroit. Among the troops stationed there were a number of interested British Masons. Together with certain residents of the town, they petitioned the Grand Lodge of New York for a Charter. In response to this petition, a warrant was issued by Grand Master Harrison, authorizing the organization of a lodge to be known as Detroit No. 337. In 1826, there were four lodges in the Territory of Michigan and a Grand Lodge was regularly organized with General Lewis Cass as the first Grand Master. Almost immediately the Masons of the Territory had to pass through the fire of bitter persecution. Their relation to the New York Grand Lodge made the hostility against them unusually bitter. In 1829, the Grand Lodge resolved to suspend labor. How little the Masons of the subordinate lodges were disturbed, is indicated by the Minutes recording the close of Zion Lodge almost on the very night when the Grand Lodge voted to suspend labor. "March 23, 1829, Zion Lodge prosperously closed;—on motion, closed in harmony. G. Hurd, Secretary."

Nothing more for eleven years! In that time, Michigan had grown into a State; its population had increased from twenty thousand to two hundred and fifty thousand. Devoted Masons were taking fresh courage and began to search for missing working tools, abandoned Altars and scattered records. At Mt. Clemens on November 13, 1840, a group of Masons met together to consider the possibility of reviving the activities of the bodies. A Committee was appointed to consider: "1. As to the existence of any Grand Lodge, heretofore or present. 2. As to the powers and duties of Master Masons who propose to associate themselves under the name and style of 'The Grand Lodge of Michigan.'"

This Committee reported that the old Grand Lodge had received its civil charter from the legislature of Michigan Territory, and was still existent as a legitimate Grand Lodge. A Convention met on June 2, 1841, in accordance with the Committee's report; opened a Master Mason's lodge, and then and there proceeded to the election of officers of the Grand Lodge of Michigan; Le Cook of Detroit being chosen Grand Master. The Convention adjourned to meet as a Grand Lodge, at Pontiac on June 24, 1841, when the officers previously chosen were duly installed. The lodges of the jurisdiction then proceeded to an orderly and busy life. But the other Grand bodies, while expressing warm admiration for the zeal and fidelity of the Masons of Michigan, could not recognize this irregularly organized body. A regular Masonic body must receive its warrant from some duly authorized and competent jurisdiction. The officers of the so-called Grand Lodge of Michigan were encouraged to proceed in the orderly way. The records of the Grand Lodge of New York contain this significant item: "Annual Meeting, 1844, the application for the revival of the three lodges warranted by this Grand Lodge in the State of Michigan, was hailed with pleasure and it was recommended that the charters for Detroit, Zion and Oakland lodges be furnished without charge." On September 11, 1844, representatives of these lodges met in Detroit, the same Grand Officers in attendance, and for the third time the Grand Lodge of Michigan was organized. This time to continue its course in unbroken activity and authority, and beneficent usefulness unto this present hour.

CHAPTER XI
Some Reflections

WHEN one considers the far-reaching effects of the Morgan incident he is profoundly impressed by this perilous possibility, that a great fraternity, founded on enduring principles of morality and brotherhood, could thus have been brought low by vilification and abuse. The conviction grows that its only security and protection is the moral integrity and unimpeachable character of its individual members. Tested by fiery persecution, glamor and glitter all faded away; and the great numerical strength melted like a snowball in the summer sunshine. Masonry survived because of the inherent and genuine worth of its spirit and principles; because of the solidity and reality of the manhood that had been builded by its precepts and maxims so constantly reiterated—the fear of God; love of the brotherhood; the honoring of civil magistrates and obedience to the law of the land. The philosophy of Masonry is not learned in a day nor in a year; nor, alone, in listening to the words of the ritual and the charges. The lodge is not a club, but a class room, in which virtue and rectitude of conduct are inculcated; a laboratory, where tolerance and brotherhood and charity are practiced. It is a great educator, intended to broaden men's minds, to enlarge their powers for good, to bring them together in the bonds of that spirit of fraternity, which alone can lighten the toil and burden of the day, as we make our pilgrim journey toward that "House not made with hands eternal in the heavens." Masonry endured and revived because it was worthy to live; if it had been false and corrupt, its decay would have been final; and its dormancy would have been the sleep of death. Masonry is a great historic fellowship of lovers of mankind—of loyal citizens of the state—of devoted seekers after Truth and after God Himself.

The experience of chastening, herein recounted, makes so plain that he who runs may read that our Temple of Masonry must be builded on Righteousness and Integrity and Honor, on Reverence for God and love of men; else when the storm descends and the floods come, its foundations shall be swept away and our Temple be brought, crashing in ruins, to the ground. Masonry is the silent partner in the home, the Church and the school, working in season and out of season, for worthier men, for happier children, for more honored and contented women. It seeks to build the Commonwealth in Wisdom, Strength and Beauty.

The Mason, if he understands his mission, is a Builder; not now of cathedrals and castles, poems in marble and granite; but builder of human society, whose stones are living men; their wild passions brought into subjection to the will of God; their minds enlightened with divine truth; their hearts made radiant with the discovered joy of pure love; their souls cherishing the immortal hope.

Never did humanity more sorely need such Builders. Doubt and discontent play upon the passions of mankind, like winds that sway the treetops in the forest. The Republic is imperiled by the seductions of luxury; by the greed for wealth and power; and by impatience with all discipline and restraint. Ignorance blinds men and leaves them susceptible to every suggestion of evil and folly; it makes men the dupes of designing demagogues preaching their gospel of anarchy and unrest. The World War left the free institutions of the world reeling from its shock. There are propagandists of every kind, political and religious, who are assailing the very foundations of our liberties, laid at such cost of life and conflict by our Masonic forefathers.

While such conditions endure, Masonry has her plain mission of service to mankind and her duty to our beloved land. Faithful to the ancient charges which forbid the introduction of questions of politics and religion for discussion within the lodge, Masonry interests itself in every phase of life that concerns the great brotherhood of mankind. It defends with all its power and influence the principle of religious liberty, of separation of church and state; and resents the intrusion, by any church, of whatever name, of its dogmas and interests and claims, into governmental departments, seeking to influence legislative, judicial or executive action. It labors to equip its own members with knowledge to understand the duties of citizenship and to appreciate its blessings; and, at the same time, intelligently to maintain and defend them. It also stands four-square for the extension of that same knowledge to the youth of the nation, our future citizens. To this end, it supports the American Public School and demands that the system be maintained at the highest degree of efficiency, under the sole dominion of the State, without interference from any political or ecclesiastical power.

If Masonry shall faithfully keep its ideals and follow the gleam of its time-honored principles, it will serve well this generation and others yet to come; and preserve for its sons the respect and the confidence of a grateful nation.

> Thou, My Country, write it on Thy heart!
> Thy sons are they, who nobly do their part.
> Who dedicates his manhood at thy shrine,
> Wherever born, is born a child of thine.
>
> And should the storms descend
> What fortress shall defend
>   The land our fathers wrought for,
> The liberties they fought for?
> What bulwark shall secure her shrines of law,
>   And keep her founts of justice pure?
> Ah then, as in the olden days,
>   *The Builders* must upraise
> A rampart of indomitable men.
> And once again, Proud Order,
> If thy hand and heart be true,
> There will be building work for thee to do
> And never dying honor shall be thine
> For setting many stones in that illustrious line
> To stand unshaken in the swirling strife
>   And guard their country's honor as her life.
>   *(Adapted from VanDyke)*